SILENT BODY
VIBRANT MIND

Living with Motor Neurone Disease

PETER ANDERSON

Published by Brolga Publishing Pty Ltd
PO Box 12544 A'Beckett St Melbourne Australia 8006
ABN 46 063 962 443
email: sales@brolgapublishing.com.au
web: www.brolgapublishing.com.au

Copyright 2012 © Peter Anderson

National Library of Australia Cataloguing-in-Publication entry

    Peter Anderson
    Silent Body Vibrant Mind: Living with Motor Neurone Disease
    ISBN 9781922036506
    Mind and body.

Printed in China
Cover design by David Khan
Typeset by Wanissa Somsuphangsri

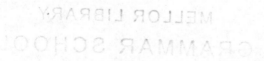

SILENT BODY
VIBRANT MIND

Living with Motor Neurone Disease

PETER ANDERSON

To Lee and Eliza,

Thanks for everything you have done for me.
You have both been everything to me.
I have loved you both on my journey
more than I could ever show.

Pete

When we sat down to write our thanks to those who have helped us over the past 11 years, we couldn't fit everyone on the page. Although the journey has been a challenging one, we have been supported and encouraged by hundreds of people; some whose role in our lives was only short, some who have walked with us the entire way. To our cherished family and friends, as well as the medical staff and carers- thank you for nurturing Pete, and our family through your unstinting care. You know who you are, and we are so grateful you have been and continue to be in our lives.

TABLE OF CONTENTS

1964 – JUNE 2001

JUNE 2001 - 2007

2011

MOTOR NEURONE DISEASE

Motor Neurone Disease (MND) is the name given to a group of diseases (i.e. Amyotrophic Lateral Sclerosis [ALS], Bulbar Palsy and Progressive Muscular Atrophy) in which the nerve cells controlling muscles of movement are slowly destroyed. These nerve cells are known as Motor Neurones and they are located in the brain and spinal cord.

With no nerves to control them the muscles gradually weaken and waste away. The weakness is often first seen in the hands, feet and throat and may be accompanied by twitching and cramps. The disease is progressive, and with time it may spread to the arms, legs and chest resulting in difficulties with speech, swallowing, breathing and general immobility.

MND is terminal, and an average course of the disease is from one to five years. However, some patients have had the disease for many years longer.

In the majority of cases the intellect and memory are not affected, nor are the senses of sight, hearing, taste, smell and sensation.

I

INTRODUCTION
by Neil Kearney, multi-award winning Australian television and newspaper journalist.

IN 2004 MARK Anderson emailed me to ask if I would write a newspaper story about his daughter Jessica's plan to walk the Kokoda Track to raise awareness of a disease afflicting Mark's brother. I feel ashamed to admit my response was so apathetic I may as well have signed it *heartless bastard.* In my email I questioned what there was to say about people cruelly struck by Motor Neurone Disease, which attacks them for no reason, and for which there is no cure. Next day I got an email from Mark's brother, Peter, containing the following:

"The story isn't in the disease, but in our triumph over it. I will succumb, but we will not be beaten. I am sure there are thousands of people like us bravely fighting their own battles in their own way, and surely that's a story worth telling".

The power of Peter's words had me imagining a powerful, vigorous man pounding furiously on a computer – but, in truth, he was so physically weakened that an email of barely a hundred words took him several painstaking hours to compose. A few hours after I received that email, I was met by Peter's wife Lee at the front door of their home in the Melbourne suburb of Box Hill.

Pete was waiting in the front room. He was propped up in a wheelchair - his only means of communication was a touch-activated voice machine. Even though he was frustrated that the conversation between Lee and I often travelled too fast for him to contribute, he still managed to convey his feelings. When Lee made a point, he emphasised it with his facial expressions – he frowned, grimaced, blinked and shook his head. When I mentioned that his email had given me a rude awakening, and that I had come in a hurry, he smirked.

From the moment we met, I was struck by the honesty of Pete and Lee. Pete's top lip was bruised, which they explained was the result of a fall in the shower earlier that week. Lee had been unable to lift him from the shower floor, so they waited 30 minutes for her father to drive from Ringwood. While Pete lay there – naked, wet, bleeding from the head and fully aware but unable to communicate – their four year-old daughter Eliza had calmly carried a succession of items to comfort him. She put her pillow under his head, fetched her Pooh bear and snuggled in alongside him to keep him warm. As Pete finished telling me that story via his touch-activated machine, his fingers hit the board excitedly. He wanted to stress how proud he was of Eliza and Lee.

At the time we met, Pete had survived three years since the diagnosis of MND – a year longer than his neurologist had predicted he would live. His friends say he has always tackled life full on. He was a fine sportsman, played golf, bowled left arm medium pace for Forest Hill, scuba-dived and surfed. The beach was his second home. He was training to run a marathon when he felt his right leg dragging slightly, the first cryptic indication of MND, a condition by which the brain stops sending messages to the muscles.

Naturally, he and Lee were devastated by the diagnosis of MND. But they had so much to live for, and had been given so little time, they refused to wallow in their grief. Pete even continued teaching for 18 months after diagnosis – until he could no longer make himself understood in the classroom.

After our first meeting, and the resultant newspaper article, Pete and I began to correspond regularly. His messages were so uplifting and profound that I created a folder to store every one. He wanted me to help him put a few sentences together, something for Eliza and Lee to keep. In his humility, he thought he needed help to get the words right.

Eliza was only 13 months old when he was diagnosed, and Pete was concerned she would remember him only as a man in a useless body. He didn't even have enough strength in his arms to hold his young daughter, and he couldn't speak or walk. He hoped he could find adequate words to tell Eliza and Lee how much he loved them.

Each time Pete wrote an article and sent it to me via email, I saved it, and then challenged him to write on another topic close to his heart – family, his early life, his passion for teaching, and so on. I figured that anyone who wrote as beautifully as he does would derive enormous pleasure from the act of putting his thoughts on paper. Writing gave him a voice - but only he and Lee knew how much pain he had to endure to express his voice.

From the outset of the writing process, he had horrific problems with his typing fingers, which became tired and raw resting in their arm splints. Just to get his body into position to write, he suffered immense discomfort that grew into agony. Each article was longer than five foolscap pages, and composing them took him countless days at the word processor. On bad days he tapped out barely a hundred words, but no amount of discomfort or tiredness thwarted him. Although the muscles were wasted badly, the tender words were strong, and the emails flowed.

About Lee:

"I look every day into her eyes and see the sheer exhaustion, frustration and agony of an uncertain future, of having the responsibilities of a single parent (as I am pretty much a lame duck in that department) and lovingly caring for me. I don't know where she finds the patience, the stamina and the will to keep giving and giving."

To Eliza:

"Don't forget to stop every once in a while and give me a fleeting thought, maybe when you're at the beach, when you are sad or in need of help. I will never be far away – there will always

be a spirit that binds us. You are a very special gift and I love you. I always will."

Of his disease:

"I feel I am a far healthier, more principled person because of this illness than I ever was before.

"I now realise that such incredible gifts have been bestowed upon me and I feel blessed.

"I know it sounds clichéd, but having the spectre of my own expiration hover over me, and the slow degeneration of my body, has stimulated a lively awareness of the goodness in the world around me and how fortunate I am to share in this life."

Even his short updates were revealing – never self-absorbed, but always truthful.

"I've had a small setback with my lungs. In five months my lung volume has fallen from 63 per cent to 38 per cent. I've done bugger all writing; I'm touching up my memorial service."

This wasn't morbidity from Pete – this was his typical frankness.

"The writing is painstakingly slow. I'm really beginning to struggle with the hands now. I need to visit the hospital to consult with the occupational therapist to get splints fitted allowing my to isolate my typing fingers as my others keep getting in the way – see what I mean!"

Heartening news:

"Great news. I'm writing again! Long story but the short of it is that an organisation called ComTEC has provided me some 'you beaut' software which allows me to produce about 10 words a minute [I'm aiming for 29 which is apparently what the average person can produce when hand-writing]. If you don't mind, may I send to you whatever I produce for your feedback?"

To be on the receiving end of Pete's emails, and to be trusted with his thoughts, is a great privilege, and one for which I am profoundly grateful. His words are so uplifting, the phrases so delicious, I have often found myself reading them out loud.

The chapters in this book are about his life before and since the diagnosis of MND – but all have been written in the years since MND took control of his body.

His writing has an irrepressible spirit. Even in the face of misery, wracked by constant pain, he has a determination to get on with life, to see the light, to grin and bear it. Only Lee and those close to him know how truly difficult his life gets, and how many times his hands have been in agony from the constant tap, tap, tap of writing.

But, true to his wish, he has fulfilled an important task – to leave his daughter Eliza with the story of her father's life, and a permanent record of his love for Eliza and Lee.

Yet he has achieved more than that. He has touched the hearts of all who read his story, for to know Pete Anderson is to be inspired by him. This book reminds us that a brave heart and strong mind can triumph even in the frailest of stricken bodies, and that greatness lies within us all.

Pete Anderson is a hero. But I daresay that is not how he would want you to regard him.

He would simply say that there are thousands of people like him bravely fighting their own battles in their own way, and that's a story worth telling.

Neil Kearney
April 2011

PROLOGUE
NO PAIN... YADDA, YADDA, YADDA

2005

I OFTEN ASK myself why I'm bothering to write on these pages. After all, it's not as if anybody is interested in what I have to say. Nor do I have any earth shattering secrets to unleash. My writing is not by any means a 'kiss and tell' attempt at titillating the senses or an endeavour to clear my conscience. I have never attempted such a task before and, as is plainly obvious, do not possess any extraordinary wit, literary intellect or story telling knack.

So why all the drudgery – all the sleepless nights mulling over my story when nobody is likely to read it? All the laborious and painful hours spent over a keyboard in the early days. My arms supported by braces and my fingers in splints to save me from hitting numerous keys at once. Those terribly dark and lonely days when I had just given up work and was struggling to come to terms with the prognosis I had been given. When my entire existence had been shaken to its core and I was seeking meaning from that terrible reality. And in the latter days, when the going was so slow, all I could manage was a miserly 100 words in a 5 hour session using my on-screen keyboard and my mouse – click, click, click. My arms too withered, tired and stiff to permit me to negotiate my fingers around a conventional keyboard until a gem of a computer program called 'Dasher' was introduced to me by the wonderful people at ComTEC Yooralla. I was at the end of my tether and had all but given up on my writing, but now I was able to again make headway – I still only went in ebbs and flows but was making progress.

Why? I guess initially it was something for me to do – something to wile away the hours when my wife Lee was at work and I was at a loose end. I have never been good at being idle. I need constant stimulation, to be involved in something bigger than myself. This has been one of the foremost challenges I have had to confront these last few years as my physical capacity has gradually diminished. I have had to become accustomed to living life between my ears. Thankfully I have never been a gregarious type of chap who craves the company of others all the time, a completely extroverted type who needs to feed off and gain energy from others. There is no doubt that I am a more introverted character and receive energy from reflection rather than action. That's not to say I am necessarily shy, retiring or antisocial!

Very soon writing became a labour of love and occupied my mind every minute of every day. Writing was on the verge of an obsession and I needed a fix regularly.

I had some things to say and did not particularly care if anybody was listening. My writing was my therapy and healing – I was writing for me. It was purely a cathartic and liberating process and at first I didn't much care who was listening, hence the initially disorganised, confused and shambolic nature of my writing that any self-respecting English teacher would probably frown upon.

One person that is particularly deserving of a note of thanks in helping me organise those ramblings into something more like an autobiography for family and friends, is journalist Neil Kearney who has encouraged me along the journey. He came to know Lee, Eliza and I through two different articles he wrote about our story for the Saturday Herald Sun several years ago. When he came to meet with us, I mentioned that I had completed some writing. He asked to see it and encouraged me to continue. He has provided counsel, suggested topics about which to write and has become a mate with whom I have conversed regularly. I trust him with my deepest, darkest stuff and he has never been judgemental or condescending about anything I have written. I need to thank him for rescuing my sanity and encouraging me to do what I never thought I had the capacity to do. He gave me two extraordinary gifts – personal growth and fulfilment, two things I did not feel I had in me when I was diagnosed with this cursed disease.

I suppose I had Eliza in mind when I first started to think about pulling all my writing together into some sort of memoir. Originally I thought that I had two, maybe three years of shelf life to produce something for Eliza to remember her pedigree and where she came from. It was an attempt to try to leave something behind through which she could get to know me. You must bear in mind that I was given a very bleak initial prognosis in 2001 and Eliza was only one year old.

It's a terribly lonely place to be when one can't communicate and I detest it. There have been times when I felt so isolated and desolate, so cut off from everyone else, I have considered, just for a fleeting moment, ending all the suffering and cashing in my chips. Then I remember all the positives in my life and get a reality check.

I feel so acutely now the sense of not being able to contribute anything to anyone and it frustrates me dreadfully. Everyone gives so much to me and I can't give anything in return but for a few empty words slowly tapped out on my LightWriter. Even the look on my face suggests that I am discontented, but that is because my facial muscles contort and spasm leaving me with the look of someone who resembles a cat's bum, when in fact, I feel emotionally quite at ease.

In July 2005, Lee, my beautiful daughter Eliza and I went away with our dear friends, Marty and Jacqui McKenna and their kids to Mount Martha on Victoria's Mornington Peninsula. Everyone was jumping through hoops for me and I was consumed by an overwhelming sense of inadequacy. I'm embarrassed to say that I actually felt sorry for myself, an emotion I rarely afford myself the luxury of feeling. I wanted to spare them (and I) the ignominy of becoming my 'carers' instead of my friends and it was a bitter pill to swallow. I felt ashamed and embarrassed. It's bad enough for Lee to be placed in this position but it's another thing entirely for friends to assume this role.

So my writing became a means of communication, a way to be heard. It was therapy for the mind and spirit. A means by which I could purge myself of all the shit built up over many nights of tossing and turning, the kind of crap you'd normally be able to discuss with your partner or your mates. My writing was also an opportunity to vent my spleen. It provided a way to clinically reconstruct in my mind and document how and when I began feeling the effects of MND.

As a teacher I encouraged my students to keep a journal and write in it regularly. In fact, I'd often pencil journal writing into the planning of my teaching schedule, so worthwhile did I consider it to be. I believed it would provide my kids an opportunity to process the daily occurrences of their lives and provide some meaning for them if they chose to really get down and dirty and open themselves up to the possibility of growth. I did not however, keep one myself, being a case of 'do as I say and not as I do'. Better late than never, I suppose.

Despite being out of the classroom for many years now I continue to miss it every single day. My work was so important to me and it essentially defined who I am. While I haven't physically taught since 2002, my passion for the work of a teacher has never waned nor has my desire to continue writing of my own experiences from my own outlook. Sitting in front of my computer, I relished the opportunity to convey my creative writing across a range of issues, free from the lingo of education speak, welfare speak or HR speak. When I have been able to summon the enormous energy required to type over the past eight years, I have been able to write freely without the shackles of convention and expectation.

I wrote about my journey, from fear to acceptance, and a comprehension that I will probably always be oscillating between the two. I came to an insight that I have much for which to be thankful – loyal and giving friends, a beautiful family, as well as a gorgeous wife and child who love me to death.

Then there's the deeper stuff. Things that I'd be loath to share with anyone about my fears, my prayers and my soul. The private, innermost thoughts that I wouldn't share with Lee for fear of frightening her - or fear of her losing all hope. Perhaps I underestimate her but I really need her to believe that I can fight this disease. Anyway, I am from the old school and want to feel that I'm protecting her from the devastation of this bloody disease, when in fact, she sees most clearly the way it continues to ravage my body. I laid myself bare, plunged into the deepest recesses of my essence and came out with an intimate understanding of who I am. In all its mundane ordinariness, it has been a beautiful life.

This is why I have persevered with my writing, because throughout the process I have developed an understanding of who I am and what I am about. This is what my writing has given me, an understanding that there are many people in this world who are worse off than me, an enhanced comprehension of my importance and place in the grand scheme of things, and an acceptance of my destiny. All the toil and hard work has been worth it. Whoever first uttered the words 'no pain, no gain' must have been a writer.

I have learnt so many things about the world around me and my place within it and how important it is to celebrate every moment of existence. I have realised that I am a reflection of other people's love and how absolutely dependent on this love I am. I have grasped that I'm a good person and have lived a full and fortunate life. Above all else, I have learnt that life is indeed not a practice run and we have to grab hold of every morsel and wring its neck.

There's nothing particularly ennobling about the journey I have had to travel these last few years. Suffering of itself does not stimulate change and growth but it does permit it. In striving while suffering, we move beyond ourselves – whether the striving attains what we set out to accomplish or not. What I mean to say is that I adore my life. This illness, though not defining me, has allowed a degree of introspection and even now as I awkwardly fumble and scratch my way through life, I feel incredibly blessed by what God has given me. That's why I implore you not to think for one moment that I will be better off when my struggle is at an end. I haven't really experienced hardship at all, at least not by any world scale of human suffering. I can't imagine what it would be like to lose a child to illness, famine or sinister means - that is to suffer. I want to continue squeezing every possible milligram out of life.

Yes, my perseverance, resilience and faith have been tested but we all have our crosses to bear. I harbour no fear for my faith tells me I will enter eternal life; only a heart-rending sense of torment because there's a great deal of unfinished business. I have fought the good fight, but *whenever* my time is up, be it next year, 10 years or maybe 20 years from now, I will be content that I have left behind a legacy. I am a good person and have touched many hearts. What more can one ask?

CHAPTER 1

MUM AND DAD

I WAS BORN in 1964 in Melbourne, the third child of Margaret and Vin. At that stage I had an elder brother Mark who was four, and a sister Donna who was two. Three years later I would have another brother Matt, while baby Phillip came along when I was 6.

Mum and Dad were both primary school teachers, although Dad's ill health – he had suffered severe depression for a number of years – made him more vulnerable to the pressures of the classroom. He retired in his mid forties. Musically, Dad was a particularly talented man with a fine ear. He was more than proficient with a keyboard and guitar (both of which he had never been taught) and highly skilled with the saxophone. As a child Dad played with his sisters in various music competitions and as a young man in a number of bands around town. Mum often speaks of the nights she would watch him playing in Town Halls throughout the city. My only recollection of Dad playing professionally was in a band called the *Forest Hillbillies*. As the name might suggest, they were a 'bush band' and Dad played the bush base. The bush base was an interesting instrument, fashioned from a large wooden tea chest with a broom handle protruding from the top. A piece of string or twine running from the top of the handle to the centre of the upturned chest would make a deep *boom boom* sound when plucked. Dad would control the notes emanating from the instrument by pulling the top of the broomstick thereby placing tension on the string.

Dad enjoyed all forms of music from classical to rock, but I must say I never saw him listening to folk music, the type he would play in the Forest Hillbillies. It seemed to me that he was playing in the band more out of a sense of service than for pure fulfilment. I suppose this tended to sum Dad up as he was really a very kindly man, deeply sensitive and always trying to please others. He was extremely gentle and lived life through his children. He wasn't particularly close to any of us, in the sense that none of us really knew him intimately, but he took a keen interest in our achievements, be they sporting, scholastic, social or professional.

Dad was never a 'performer'. He hated the limelight and I remain convinced that the pressure placed on him to perform, particularly by his mother, was the primary cause of the number of psychological breakdowns he was to endure. Music was an escape for him and never intended as a vehicle for his ego. As he got older, music became a barometer of his mental state. When he was feeling at ease with himself and the world, we would find him sitting at the organ, strumming a guitar or listening to music on his quadraphonic stereo. The Andersons were the only people I knew who could boast such a stereo system – not that anyone else cared!

On the bad days, which seemed to occur far more regularly than the good, Dad wouldn't usually be seen before dinner-time. As time went by, the pressures of everyday life just became too much for him. More and more he would not surface before late afternoon and on numerous occasions Mum would take his dinner upstairs. These invariably remained untouched and in the early hours of the morning I would wake to the sound of Dad raiding the pantry for any morsel he could get his hands on. When Dad did make it down for dinner, conversation at the table was fairly limited for fear of invoking Dad's scorn. The family would tread very carefully around the business of the day ensuring there was no controversy or dissension, thereby trying to avoid conflict with him.

As we grew older, however, and battled adolescence, such conflict became inevitable, and on some occasions, even welcomed. From my perspective, I was becoming angry at the impact Dad was having on my family and me. He was retreating further and further into himself and I had little sympathy for his tormented state. I hated seeing him so feeble and seemingly ill-equipped to deal with life's vagaries. I had little understanding of what he was going through and little inclination to try. I was annoyed and sometimes even embarrassed by his behaviour. It is so ironic now that I find myself in exactly the same position; battling to extricate myself from bed, weakened by illness, housebound, feeble and becoming increasingly dependent on others. I sometimes even wonder if I am perhaps being punished for my insensitivity and lack of empathy for what Dad was going through. He didn't want to be the way he was and was clearly tormented, as I am, by his inability to live a 'normal' life. His disease was psychological but no less real or debilitating than mine.

The time of his death in 1999 was a remarkable period for the family and in a way galvanised our love and affection for one another. It was a defining moment for us, bringing us closer together, the way I always wanted us to be. It also gave us the chance to demonstrate publicly our esteem, love and affection for Dad and allow him the peace he so eagerly sought in the later stages of life.

I learnt so much from my mother during my childhood – not that I realised it then. I cannot remember a single occasion when Mum spoke ill of my father, though sometimes she had every reason to. The embodiment of the Christian ideal, she lived out these values in all aspects of her life. A person of immense inner strength and eternal optimism, she suffered more than her fair share throughout her marriage but never once complained about the way things could have been. Her love for Dad was obvious and the harder life grew, the more devoted she became. When Dad was seriously ill after his numerous strokes, his personality changed quite drastically and he often lashed out verbally and sometimes physically, especially towards Mum but also on occasion towards nursing staff and other members of the family. We would often say to Mum, 'if he's going to behave like that, don't go and visit him.' Mum would simply respond by reciting her wedding vows, 'in sickness and in health, in good times and in bad.'

Mum was the rock on which we could always rely. Although she worked full-time in a highly demanding role as a teacher, she also undertook a Bachelor of Special Education and found the time to care for a family of seven. She was highly respected in her profession and became a leader in her field – providing integration support in a mainstream educational environment for intellectually and mentally disabled children. To this day, I have the utmost admiration and respect for who and what she is. I love the way she sees only the good in people and refuses to let circumstances get her down. Even her own battle with cancer failed to dent her spirit. I draw much of my own strength from her.

CHAPTER 2

THE CONTEST

F ROM A YOUNG age I always sought a contest – a chance to test my mettle and use it as a measure of my own ability, perseverance and skill. While I enjoyed meeting a good competitor, from my very early days it was all about the contest of sport.

My love of sport can be credited to my Mum – she's a fanatic. Mum's cousin is Australian Rules Football star Phonse Kyne; Collingwood Magpies captain and coach, three-time winner of the club's coveted best and fairest E.W. Copeland Trophy and member of their Team of the Century. Mum shared many stories of those heady days – she and Phonse used to travel by tram to his games in Melbourne every Saturday and she knew each of the players personally. She spoke the names of Robert 'Bob' Rose, Lewis 'Lou' Richards, Neil Mann and Murray Weideman in reverent terms, like she was speaking about the Gods. I guess in her mind she was. (Still a passionate supporter of her beloved Pies, she goes to the footy every week and at 75, that's not a bad effort. As a member of the Collingwood Social Club, she attends their Club Night at the Lexus Centre in Melbourne once every month). Hence we shouldn't have been surprised that Mum followed our sporting careers religiously, as did my sister, Donna. Whether it was a freezing Saturday morning at the local footy, a sweltering afternoon scoring at the cricket or 10.30pm at the Box Hill Indoor Cricket Centre to cheer on the 'Pheasant Pluckers', we could always rely on Mum to support us from the stands and cart us off to hospital when the need arose. She spent many an hour in emergency wards around the country.

My vibrant, rich memories of sport go back as far as early primary school. I remember nervously getting ready for football in front of the fire on freezing mornings while watching *Hey Hey It's Saturday*. We had to wear Geelong Football Club jumpers because our parish priest barracked for the Cats. Rain, hail or shine I would run to school, making sure to stay on the nature strips and jump every driveway between home and school for fear of wearing down the stops on my authentic Ron Barassi footy boots. Our coach, Mr Wilder, would give every kid a run, no matter their ability, so long as they had been to training. When he awarded me the trophy for best clubman, I was overcome with pride and humility. Of all the trophies I've been given, this is the one I most treasure because of what it represents and the reason for which it is awarded. He was always positive when he addressed us and took an interest in us individually, finding ways to congratulate us for what seemed then to be pretty insignificant acts.

These days in the Australian Football League (AFL), these acts are called the 'one percenters'– the small efforts of applying pressure which make opposition turnovers more likely. There is no doubt Mr Wilder was both ahead of his time and a huge influence on my life.

I lived and breathed sport. Or, should I say, I lived and breathed physical activity. Nothing was done without a ball in my hand and the same was true of everyone I knew. We lived in a long court and played with gay abandon for hours on end. We'd play whole test cricket matches and four quarters of football. The sound of a bouncing football would bring every kid from the surrounding streets out of their homes as if they were being summoned to prayers in a mosque. If there was nobody to play with you'd play by yourself, kicking the footy between the tree and the lamp post or bowling a tennis ball into the garage door. If that didn't bring someone running, nothing would! I used to sharpen my reflexes by taking slips catches for hours on end against the side of the house, which must have driven Mum and Dad to distraction. We played our test cricket matches in the Howells' next door. Murray, Gary and Jeff lived there, and the rivalry was pretty keen. Their father's name was Don and he would cast a critical eye over our games. If we lofted the ball, he'd grumble and berate us, 'Along the carpet; always along the carpet.' If we bowled a bouncer he'd mumble to keep the ball on a good length, 'Up at his toes', he'd say. If you tried to thrash a ball to off or leg you'd hear, 'Play in the vee mate, always in the arc'. I didn't realise then that Don Howell was responsible for developing some fundamental skills and important habits in my cricket.

My big brother Mark was my under 14s and under 16s coach at the Forest Hill Cricket Club in Melbourne's eastern suburbs. He used to have a lot of faith in my ability, maybe too much, and often asked me to open the batting. Either that or he was getting one back for my adolescent assuredness. I couldn't tell him that I was packing myself and had to swallow the lump in my throat many times. In hindsight, he was giving me opportunities to succeed, but I didn't see them as such. I hated facing the new ball. In the old junior days we played on hessian matting and the new ball used to rear up at you and make a hissing sound as the air flicked the seam. I was struck many times, but in the end you just had to wear them and grit your teeth.

After my juniors' days, I graduated to grade cricket and I distinctly remember a grand final I played in the Thirds against Blackburn in 1986. We lost the toss but strangely they sent us in to bat, an unusual thing to do in the circumstances – but their strategy became clear. They had a bowler who was making his way back from injury who would normally be in the Firsts. He was devilishly quick and as mean as hell. I don't think he knew where he was going to put each ball and we certainly had no clue how to combat his pace. Before long we were four wickets down for not much and struggling against his pace.

I went in and didn't see the first three or four deliveries he sent down. He had an unusual action. It was very difficult to pick up the release of the ball because he brought his arm from behind his body at the last second and had a fast slinging action. In short, I had no idea! These were the times when in grade cricket helmets were rarely seen and, in fact, to wear one was courting danger and much derision. It simply gave the bowler something to aim at and you could bank on a barrage from the slips fieldsman about your lineage and sexual orientation. I had managed to see him off and scratched around for an hour or so, eking out 30 runs in the process.

Unfortunately they brought him back for a quick and hostile burst before tea.

First up he sent a beam ball down that thundered into the fleshy part of my upper thigh. Before the stinging sensation hit I voiced my displeasure at being bowled such a ball, but then the pain set in. It was all I could do not to rub it but - against my better judgment - I did so. He needed no further invitation and, true to form, delivered the next one directly at my head. I should have been expecting it but you always assume the ball will bounce. When it is nowhere to be seen you begin pushing panic buttons, start to duck and protect your head. That's exactly what I did as the hard red cherry loomed large, crashing into my wrist only millimetres from my face and glancing off my head. Immediately, my wrist swelled up to the size of a melon and was extremely sore. I batted out the few remaining overs until tea and sought an ice-pack during the interval. We won that final, in no small part due to my steadying innings, and my resolve both surprised and pleased me. It was one of those defining moments on the playing field where you really learn who you are, your character is tested and thankfully, I did not find myself wanting.

I have so many wonderful memories of my times spent chasing, hitting and kicking a ball. Not memories of being triumphant or receiving accolades, but more overt recollections and deep-rooted reminiscences, the kind that have had a greater impact on the person I've become. The sporting arena is the ideal training ground for life and it is here you can make mistakes without catastrophic consequences. So many lessons are learnt there – how to cope with disappointments, perseverance, humility, the value of hard work, social skills, playing by the rules, and personal conduct.

CHAPTER 3

MORE THAN A JOB

TEACHING IS A noble profession and I was fortunate that from the relatively young age of 16 or 17 I settled on it as a choice of career. Mum and Dad were both primary school teachers, so the seed was probably sown when I was even younger. Also, considering my personality is naturally quite introspective and reflective, it was inevitable that I would end up in a nurturing and caring type of vocation.

Prior to my senior secondary years I had not been a particularly productive or conscientious student. There seemed little point really, as I knew I could catch up when it really mattered. I was very quiet and never felt comfortable enough to speak up in class. I rarely did so unless prompted. Then I would turn a bright shade of crimson and splutter a monosyllabic answer.

Mind you, the learning environment was not exactly conducive to fostering a sense of self-confidence amongst classmates. My year level had its fair share of dominant thugs who did all in their considerable power to quell any meaningful discussion of issues or make one feel comfortable in risking ridicule by asking questions and appearing interested. In the face of such odds I decided to lie low and play it cool, much the same as hundreds of thousands of kids presently sitting in Australian classrooms. I lay the blame not at the feet of those domineering kids, as they probably didn't know any better, but on the teachers who lacked the skills or the balls to shift the emphasis back to the masses. Later it became my mission to give these kids a voice and subdue the thugs, attention mongers and smart arses to create the learning environment I so craved.

As I reflect on what led me to seriously pursue a career as a chalkie, it was almost certainly two very different yet equally skilful teachers who aroused my desire to follow in their footsteps. Danny Kennelly was my Year 12 Australian History and Legal Studies teacher. He had a huge personality and kept us entertained for hours on end with his frenetic energy and quirky sense of humour. I am sure he was quite mad and, as is typical with such 'up' people, his ups were hilariously funny but his lows were at the other end of the spectrum, depressive and morose. Rumour has it that he would often arrive in the staffroom bearing flowers as an apology for having flown off the handle at a member of staff over some inane issue. He left you with no uncertainty as to how he was feeling on any particular day, but for me this all added to the excitement of being in his classes. Above all, however, he cared deeply about his students and gave totally of himself and his time. Not only did he seek to know us, but he shared with us parts of his own life, his loves, aspirations and desires. We came to know him more intimately than we had ever previously been allowed into a teacher's life. It was clear that he placed his faith in us and we began to grow as people within this environment of trust. We could share things with one another, speak about matters of the heart, depend on one another and learn in an environment where mutual respect and understanding were the fabric of our relationships. I thrived in this setting and loved coming to school.

Peter Molinari was my Year 11 and 12 Economics teacher. He and Danny were close friends. Peter had a dry and cutting wit and ran his classes with a firm hand. He was uncompromising and, on the surface, lacking any compassion in his dealings with us. He was relentless and had very high expectations of all those in his class.

His dictum was 'if you don't like it; leave'. If you weren't adequately prepared for class he'd be dismissive and ignore you for the lesson and if you'd handed in work that was below par, he'd lambaste you and throw it back in your face.

On a few occasions this approach didn't go down too well with various female members of the class. Some stormed out in fits of rage or tears of torment. On such occasions, Peter's exterior betrayed no sense of remorse as he quietly closed the door behind the wailing student and continued teaching in the same tone as before the calamitous scene. However, we knew by the enormous number of hours he spent with us that he cared; after school, at lunchtime and over the holidays in preparation for our exams. He gave 100 per cent and expected the same in return – nothing more, nothing less. I don't recall being late with any work and was certainly punctual to class. He extracted more out of me than I ever thought possible.

Peter and Danny plied their trade very differently yet both had a profound impact on me and my progression towards a career in teaching and, more importantly, my journey towards manhood. They demonstrated enormous energy, enthusiasm and love for what they were doing – and they were brilliant at it. Above all, they made me feel special, not by blowing wind up my backside, but in their encouragement for me to succeed, believing in me and supporting me, each in their own way.

I would like to think that I later successfully adopted much of their approach into my teaching. In fact, it was largely due to these two that in my final year of schooling I sought, and achieved, a student leadership position as a College Captain. Given that two years prior I was seeking anonymity, too afraid to raise my hand for fear of failure and derision, this was an enormous leap forward for me.

I graduated from secondary school in 1982 and attended La Trobe University in Melbourne, where I studied a Bachelor of Arts, with majors in Legal Studies and Politics and a minor in Sociology. My sister Donna had recently completed a similar course and spoke highly of it. She had lived on campus in the dorms and thoroughly enjoyed the whole university experience whereas I could not bring myself to embrace the university existence. I did not utilise the facilities that such an enormous institution has to offer and did not seek to make friends - but for a few individuals on a cordial basis.

I did not avail myself of these things because I was in a relationship with a girl with whom I had graduated from high school. We were seriously going out and spent a great deal of time together and among a small group of school friends. I was smitten by Jacinta and was convinced that she and I would spend the rest of our lives together. Alas she broke my heart and, after nearly three years, we parted company. This left me devastated and faltering in a huge, cold and lonely university where I felt very much forsaken. This all took place towards the end of my final year and I was in no condition, and had little inclination, to hit the books and study for my looming exams.

The extent of my devastation was, in hindsight, quite alarming. There were days when I'd lie on my bed and cry like a baby into my pillow. I found myself driving past her house to see if she was home and dropping in on her and her parents. Of course, during such visits I was outwardly beaming and regaling them with stories of how well I was doing in my cricket, at university and in life generally. I guess my hope was that she'd tell me it was all a mistake and we could resume our life together. Maybe I was also going out of my way (literally) to show her that I was a survivor and she had not mortally wounded me.

Fortunately I scraped through my exams and was successful in my application to the Australian Catholic University (ACU) to study a Graduate Diploma of Education; a one year full-time course that would enable me to teach in Catholic secondary schools. ACU (or Christ College as it was known then) was a very small institution by today's standards. It consisted of 1000 students studying Primary Teaching and my intake of graduate diploma students, comprising approximately 60 people from the major universities who had all completed a bachelor's degree. For us it was like returning to school.

Three years at university had been characterised by wasted opportunities to broaden my life experience and though I was still reeling from my break-up with Jacinta, I was determined not to let another year slip by without tasting the free and easy lifestyle of a student immersed in an existence dominated by girls, grog and good times. If the preceding years had been spiritless, this particular year could only be described as dynamic. I threw myself into all that the institution had to offer; sport, social events and even found myself elected as a graduate-student representative on the Student Representative Council. There is no doubt that I occupied myself far too much in the social side of college life to the detriment of my academic studies and lost sight of the main game. This having been said, I have absolutely no regrets about my time at ACU. Thankfully the course was not particularly rigorous, as I spent little time with my head in a book and survived by doing the absolute minimum required. I made lifelong friends from my year there and we share wonderful memories of our time together.

CHAPTER 4

COUNT TO TEN, MR ANDERSON

D URING MY GRADUATE diploma in 1986, I completed my final teaching round (a four-week period of practical experience as a student teacher) at Mount Lilydale Mercy College in Melbourne's outer east. The Principal, a formidable nun named Sister Beth, called me into her office and brusquely inquired as to why I had not applied for the Legal Studies position advertised recently in the media. I told her that I had been offered a job elsewhere and was in the process of formalising my agreement with that school. Sister Beth would have none of that and created a position for me to start the following year, which was too good to refuse. It was always too dangerous to refuse her - I had seen her pay out on various members of staff, and did not feel inclined to be on the receiving end. The teaching position consisted of senior Legal Studies, Year 10 Commerce, Year 8 Religious Education and Homeroom, and the very interesting role of running personal development camps at our beachside site in Mornington.

I could not have wished for a more challenging role and probably, on occasion, needed it to be less so. Classroom teaching is always an exacting job and being first year out of teachers' college makes it all the more demanding. But when you add to this the duties pertaining to camp organisation and leadership, you add an enormous weight in terms of responsibility, accountability and workload. The role involved driving half a class of excited students in a bus to Mornington (for which I had to get my heavy vehicle licence, pronto), running a personal development program that included ice-breaking activities, supervising free time at the beach (for which I had to get my Bronze Medallion Life Saving qualification) and stalking the corridors at all hours of the morning to ensure the kids did not 'stray' after lights out.

Over the few years I was involved in the team we developed a wonderfully diverse, challenging and exciting camp program of which I am very proud. I learnt a great deal about kids, and this provided a solid foundation for the rest of my career.

As exciting as this role was, I wanted to focus more on teaching at the senior end of the curriculum and after two years was able to drop the retreats and concentrate solely on Commerce and Legal Studies at Years 10, 11 and 12. My interpersonal skills were far better suited to these kids as I didn't have the patience with the young ones.

My five wonderful years at Mount Lilydale College were very special. As a bright-eyed graduate teacher, I threw myself headlong into the experience - without any preconceived notions or expectations, and sucked every last bit out of the place. I loved the kids and felt like I belonged. It wasn't like a job at all and in five years I only had two sick days.

Each day I arrived at least an hour before the first bell and was usually one of the last to leave. I volunteered to go on every camp, committee and extra-curricular activity. I had a policy for my corrections whereby all work handed in would be marked and corrected within two days. This placed additional pressure on me, but the kids responded well. I had equally high expectations of my students in terms of their behaviour, punctuality and work habits, but nearly always found that whatever the expectation, if given encouragement, they were able to meet it. I became a true believer in this maxim. If you set the bar low, a class, group or student will generally strive only to meet that level. If you set the bar high then, given the resources and a safety net, kids can achieve beyond their wildest dreams.

I conducted my classes strictly in terms of the level of courtesy I expected from the kids towards each other and towards me - but we had a lot of fun too. My kids came to know me well and I them. This is the most rewarding aspect of the 'job'. It's the privilege of being involved in each other's lives. I rarely raised my voice and found this worked very well because when I needed to get stern they knew I must have been pissed off. When that happened, they generally toed the line. I remember one of my lecturers saying that it's always best to lose your temper before you actually lose your temper. When this was called for, I would give the words 'pens down' in a deep, quiet voice, and outwardly seethe about a certain aspect of their behaviour, whilst trying not to laugh out loud.

On one occasion, however, this pointer went completely out the window and, if not for the timely intervention of a darling young student, would have almost certainly cost me my career. I was probably not completely on my game on the day in question and was particularly keen to keep a Year 10 Commerce class under a tight rein. I wasn't pleased with their general behaviour and found myself putting out spot fires throughout the room.

They weren't on-task and this annoyed me to the point where I began to take it personally. I had spent a great deal of time planning and preparing this lesson and they were damn well going to listen, absorb and take part, even if it was last period on a Friday.

If I had been more experienced, I would have known to adapt the task or have read the early signs and not have introduced such a task in the first place. However, as my class began to fall apart, I zeroed in on the prime movers, the troublemakers, who I thought were the source of all my ills.

One boy in particular had me in a spin and I was determined not to have him 'butcher' my class. I kept my eye on him and immediately pounced on his next transgression, a minor one in the scheme of things. I gave him the most severe spray, which was out of all proportion for the behaviour he had exhibited.

Tirade over, I was about to resume teaching when a barely audible 'get fucked' came from the back of the room.

Well, the whole class froze…. and awaited my reaction. It was obvious where the comment originated from, and I was absolutely furious.

Worse, I was out of control, white hot and looking for retribution.

How could he speak to me like that? It was my perception that my credibility as a self-respecting teacher had evaporated before their very eyes.

I screamed at him, 'GET OUTSIDE, NOW!'

I was in such a rage that I followed him from the room and would, I am sure, have put him through a bank of lockers. At the precise moment I approached the door, a student called Samantha, an angel sitting near the doorway said quietly, 'Count to ten, Mr Anderson', and immediately brought me back to my senses.

Everything had been spinning out of control, but her gentle words infused in me a calmness and a perspective dangerously lacking to this point in time. I was still as angry as hell, but I was under control and able to rationally deal with the kid. I have no doubt that if Sam had not intervened I would have violently reacted to this boy in a way that would have had serious recriminations. Interestingly, he too knew how close to the wind he had sailed and was genuinely frightened by the experience. Although a challenging student, we shared a close relationship after that. I later informed Sam of how thankful I was.

I learnt a valuable lesson that day and never again allowed myself to spiral into a similar situation. I was to blame for the lesson getting out of control. I had prepared a lesson that involved group work and discussion at a time when the kids, 30 15-year-olds, were thinking only of their weekend and were not capable of remaining on-task. I let the situation escalate into one where I was forced to address the serious issue of a student swearing at a teacher rather than adequately addressing the primary issue of him not doing his work. I followed him from the room rather than provide space that gave us both the opportunity to cool down. I was lucky to come out of the lesson relatively unscathed. Yes, a lesson learned.

I still see or receive emails from many of the kids from that era and am proud of the input I had into their lives. It's great to hear of their successes in work and in their family lives. There was something special about that time, an intangible spirit about the people who all came together for a common purpose – the kids in our care. Around the same time that I was employed, there were many other graduate teachers. This injected exuberance into the college and what we lacked in experience we made up for with enthusiasm. We were guided by excellent leaders who gave us enough latitude to really make a difference, but also supported us when our judgement was off the mark. I often sought the counsel of wiser, more experienced heads and carried their advice with me throughout my career. It's such a wonderful experience to be in an institution where everyone (or the majority) is pulling in the one direction. I believe this to be the single most important factor in our success over this period, and the biggest contributor to their ongoing achievements. We all believed in what we were attempting to achieve; happy kids, a safe and comfortable environment, and a workplace that was enjoyable to be in.

One of the many personally challenging aspects of my early days as an educator was that I was required to teach my brother, Phillip. He had just completed a technical Year 12 course at my old school, Emmaus College, but decided he wanted to join the police force, thus requiring the more traditional Victorian Certificate of Education. Obviously, with my contacts at Mount Lilydale, he was a shoo-in to be accepted. Unfortunately his choice of subjects meant that he had to be in my Year 12 Legal Studies class which, I might add, was the first time I had taught the subject at this level.

At this stage I was still living at home and so shared the house with him, sat across the same dinner table and was acutely aware of the quantity of homework he was (or wasn't) doing. This actually put great strain on our relationship because, and I'm sure Phil would concur, he was not the most diligent of students. It must have been very difficult for him with me breathing down his neck every night; and I was less than subtle in voicing my disapproval when he was going out or just relaxing in front of the TV. He handled the situation with his usual dismissive humour and my concerns were like water off a duck's back.

Phil knew how to put me back in my box and was never reluctant to do so, no matter what the situation or setting. I like to include examples to illustrate concepts and ideas when I teach and was scratching for one when teaching Constitutional Law. From the recesses of my mind I dragged up a case I remembered my dad talking about involving my grandmother and her fight for compensation with the government after the death of my grandfather. I called the case Anderson vs the Commonwealth and I didn't let the truth get in the way of making my point.

I caught out of the corner of my eye a raised hand – Phillip's. He had a wry smile on his face and I tried to ignore him as best I could. Soon the class too was aware that he had something to add - but I pressed on regardless.

Eventually, having illustrated my point, my disregard for Phil's question had become awkward. He had a broad grin on his mug and – against my better judgement – I asked the subject of his enquiry.

Phil has never been one to mince words.

'That is the biggest load of bullshit I've ever heard' he said, and proceeded to set the record straight.

I still used the example in my teaching and often had a quiet chuckle about this embarrassing incident.

As many of my old colleagues so often reminisce about the fun we had, lots of things come to mind. One was Year 7 Orientation Days when my colleagues in the Year 7 area conducted tours for the masses of Grade 6 students who were going to attend Mount Lilydale the following year. As part of the tour they would bring them in small groups to me in the Senior School and introduce me as the school's helicopter pilot who flew only the very best-behaved students to camp. It was fun to see their jaws drop at the prospect of having a ride in a helicopter but strangely, not one of them ever mentioned it the following year. This was probably because their parents set them straight that we were having a lend of them.

One event has virtually become folklore amongst those 'in the know'. A large group of us were supervising a Year 10 dance organised by the students at the local parish hall. Also manning the door was a collection of parent volunteers. Midway through the dance the disc jockey played a song by The Angels called *'Am I ever going to see your face again?'*

The students went into a frenzy, and wild expectation filled the hall – this was going to be their moment.

As the chorus boomed, 'Am I ever going to see your face again?', 200 students screamed in reply, 'No way, get fucked, fuck off', and turned to the staff in euphoric delight at our powerlessness.

In sheer embarrassment at the fact that our formidable Principal, Sister Beth, had chosen this moment to drop in, I decided that this was a good time to check how the dads were doing outside on the door. With the student chant rising to a crescendo and resonating through my head, I exited (or bailed out), and noticed that a thick fog had settled on the ground. 'Jeez, it's pretty fuckin' foggy,' I exclaimed to all and sundry. There was no hole big enough for me to jump into.

More than anything else, I loved having a homeroom class. In such an environment where you are able to break down the walls between students and teachers, you get a real insight into them as people, as brother and sisters, daughters and sons, their friendships, their loves, interests and fears. This is where the true rewards lie, because the relationship begins to take on new dimensions beyond the classroom and the confines of the college grounds. It is in the homeroom where you develop the closest ties with your students. Here you see them at the start and completion of every school day. I celebrated their birthdays, was invited to their homes, attended camps and shared aspects of my own life with them.

Further down the school in Years 7, 8 and 9, you might teach your homeroom a number of subjects as well. The homeroom is the primary avenue for pastoral care in the school and the most important unit through which the student receives a sense of belonging. It is the first point of contact between the school and the home and I had the pleasure of developing close relationships with many families during my time there. But it is also in such a setting where you experience immense anguish and pain. I lost two of my dear students in road accidents over a three-year period and still memories of them and those terribly sad times haunt me.

Emma was doing some last minute Father's Day shopping and was happily giggling with school friends when she stepped in front of a bus.

She was killed instantly.

I received news early the following day, Father's Day, and quickly rushed to meet Sister Beth at school. She told me I should go to Emma's home and offer whatever support I could. A tough call for a 22-year-old junior teacher but she was right. It was my duty to represent the college and I needed to be there.

As I arrived, the grief was overwhelming; it hung over the house like a shroud. Emma's parents rushed into my arms but I couldn't say anything except 'I'm so sorry'. What can you say to parents who have had their 16 year-old child wrenched from them? My gut churned as I witnessed their pain while we began discussing funeral arrangements and the role that Emma's school could play. As a Catholic school, the parents would rightfully rely on us to help them through this process.

The next day I arrived at school early to steel myself for the arrival of my homeroom. As they alighted their buses or were dropped off by parents, the Co-ordinator quickly whisked them into my classroom. I am not proficient enough with the pen to explain what happened in our room that morning but, suffice to say, the beauty of that moment will go with me forever. Tragically, shortly after, I was to experience many similar emotions all over again.

Jeanette Surh worked at the college reception and had become a close friend. I was drawn to her vivaciousness and sense of fun. When we learned that her daughter, Tanya, was going to be in my Year 12 Homeroom we were both delighted. Tanya shared her mum's sense of humour and was as soft as a rose. She used to sit on a desk after school waiting for mum and we'd have long chats while I was cleaning up. She was a very special kid and we shared a unique relationship.

One Saturday night late in the year she and some friends were coming home from a night out when a drunk and drugged driver ran a red light, ploughed into their car and killed Tanya. I was shattered.

Again I found myself on the doorstep of a grieving family, hugging them in the doorway with that very same black pall hanging over the once vibrant family home. And again I had to discuss a funeral for a student who had her life ahead of her, with all its unfulfilled potential. Above all, I will never forget their dignity in this time of unimaginable suffering and the way Jeanette, her husband Greg and their son Paul accepted and comforted me. In the face of their suffering I felt that it was important I hold myself together, but on the drive home I wept uncontrollably.

Jeanette asked me to speak at Tanya's funeral but I declined, fearing my inability to cope emotionally and dragging down what needed to be a dignified ceremony. But also I was concerned about not doing justice to the life of an extraordinary person. We settled on my doing the following scripture reading;

Isaiah *(25:6-9)* – The Lord God
will destroy death for ever.

On this mountain, the Lord of hosts will prepare for all peoples a banquet of rich food. On this mountain he will remove the mourning veil covering all peoples, and the shroud enwrapping all the nations, he will destroy Death for ever.

The Lord God will wipe away the tears from every cheek; he will take away his people's shame everywhere on earth, for the Lord has said so.

That day, it will be said: See, this is our God in whom we hoped for salvation; the Lord is the one in whom we hoped. We exult and we rejoice that he has saved us.

The word of the Lord.

I wish I could have spoken at the funeral because there was much I could and should have said – one of my few regrets from this time. Jeannie and I still remain in contact, and I am forever in awe of her strength and ability to reach out and touch others in her time of suffering.

CHAPTER 5

SCHOOL, SURF, SPORT

A S AN EDUCATOR there are many tools you need to use in your teaching, and often I would use sport and the many opportunities the yard and a ball presented. In senior Legal Studies classes the first thing I did for the year was direct them down to the yard and toss them a ball. I'd instruct them to play safely, but didn't give any further instructions. The big beefy boys would soon dominate and everyone else would get jack of the game. Then they'd start to introduce rules, teams and boundaries. Before long most get involved in a hybrid form of football, basketball and soccer. It was a simple and fun way to illustrate the need for laws and has never failed.

My own passion for sport only grew further throughout my twenties, and I developed a particular love for surfing. Sometimes the contest is fought within – it is waged within the confines of the mind. This is probably true of all sports but in my case it's true most of all with my surfing.

Away from the classroom, surfing became an important part of my life. I love the surf scene, the lifestyle, the freedom. I'm not suggesting that I was much good at it, on the contrary I actually stank, but that didn't stop me from trying and working at it. Many a long hour was spent floundering in the break, unable to make my way through the white water and out of harm's way, only to eventually make it out the back, paddle for a wave and get unceremoniously thumped on take-off. It would have been easy to give up, throw in the towel and retreat to the warmth of the fire. Not long before I became ill I bought an expensive boogie board and fins and it all came together. There was nothing wrong with my wave selection or strength; it was predominantly my flexibility that was the root of my problems.

We surfed a great deal at Phillip Island. My close mate Kev Logan had an uncle who was a Christian Brother and Principal at St. Bedes in Mentone. A whole troop of us used to use their retreat facilities for a few weeks every year, writing ourselves off by night and surfing all day. The place was perfectly located on the cliff overlooking Smith's Beach and the Young Catholic Workers Camp. I have many fond memories of my days there and some frightening ones too. On the odd occasion massive surf slams the coastline and when you're with a group of testosterone-charged, macho and bulletproof males, there's nowhere to hide. We chanced our luck far too often in conditions way beyond our ability or, at least, I did! On occasions I was in fear of my life and completely at the whim of nature. We did not give her due respect and should have paid the price many times. I'm not a particularly courageous surfer and when a large wave jacked up to expose a sharp reef of jagged rocks, my heart would be in my mouth. There were many times when I simply bailed out.

One event that looms largest in my mind happened at Berry's Beach on Phillip Island. It was a big day, but not huge. We decided on Berry's because everywhere else was too messy. There were six or seven of us about 200 metres from shore, laughing and having a great time, happy in each other's company. The swell was interspersed by periods of calm which gave us a chance to rest and carry on with the tomfoolery. The light was just beginning to fail as it was nearing dusk and I was starting to get very cold.

Fitzy, a big, strapping young lad, afraid of nothing and no one, had manoeuvred himself away from the group and over to our left in an attempt to get the best of the conditions. We were becalmed, the wind had ceased and eerie silence descended upon the ocean.

Just then Fitzy let out a blood curdling 'JEEESUS' and paddled over at a great rate of knots.

He said, 'Something just surfaced next to me and it had a dorsal fin, it was grey and it was fucking huge.'

We all joined hands in a circle and tried our best to keep our feet from the water. Fitzy was hanging on to my arm and up until this point I had not been overly worried. You see many things in the surf and usually it's a seal, a dolphin or a shadow on the bottom. Fitzy, however, was not prone to panic and his trembling arm had me concerned. Someone suggested that we start quietly and gently paddling in and I heard no arguments from anyone else. If a big shark was circling there was a 1 in 7 chance that it would get you. These odds were OK by me and I started to paddle.

Gently but steadily we all made headway until a wave came.

Somebody yelled, 'Every man for himself!', and not a single person missed that wave. It was funny to see us all on our bellies, chortling about how we had all cheated death.

My love of water also extended to scuba diving. I loved scuba diving. I'm not sure whether you'd class diving as a sport or a hobby but it's certainly challenging and mentally and physically demanding. People would often ask what there is to see when diving, especially when diving in Port Phillip Bay. My answer was always the same. There is as much to see there as there is to see when you look around you now. The big difference being that I am seeing everything for the first time. It's a whole new world, different creatures, different sensations and sounds. My dive master/instructor used to encourage us to dive without gloves so we could feel things when we descended. He also encouraged us to taste things like seaweed when on the bottom to immerse ourselves in the full experience.

In the days leading up to my brother Matt's wedding in Western Australia, he organised a scuba dive off Rottnest Island for my older brother Mark and I, as well as his best man, Adrian. Little did we know it was to be the most full-on experience we would all have beneath the water.

Open Water divers are only certified to a depth of 18 metres for very good reason. Once you go too far beyond that you're courting danger and have to consider decompression stops and other complications. 18 metres is still 60 feet and once you get to this depth the colours are pretty much shades of grey anyway. We were no sooner in the dive boat when Adrian started vomiting his guts out but, to his credit, he was not deterred. He simply wiped the vomit from his chin, took a swig of VB and grinned. We dropped anchor in 18 metres of water, suited up, completed our safety checks and entered the water.

The visibility was endless and the excitement was palpable. The site was teeming with fish and all manner of vegetation which rose 10 metres from the bottom. There were huge boulders and swim throughs everywhere. We were so caught up in the beauty of our surroundings we wandered into about 30 metres of water, far deeper than I had ever dived before. This didn't pose too much of a problem as long as we ascended slowly and kept an eye on our air supply.

Adrian and I had been 'buddied' up by the dive crew and Mark accompanied someone else. The buddy system works on the theory that you look out for me and I'll look out for you. I was keeping a close eye on Adrian because he was having trouble with his buoyancy, when suddenly I lost him.

He was nowhere to be seen.

I frantically searched the immediate area then looked up.

Sure enough that's where he was, battling with his buoyancy control device (BCD) again, bum-up and fighting to get down to the bottom.

The BCD operates by the transfer of air via the tank

through a valve. You can then regulate the volume of air in your vest by pressing a small button on a tube located near the chest and releasing air by pulling on the same tube to achieve neutral buoyancy. The problem poor Adrian was encountering was that he needed to be upright to jettison air through the valve he was attempting to use but he was in a bum-up position. All the air was in the bottom of his vest so he needed to use the valve situated at the bottom of his BCD. He was panicking and thrashing about trying to reach the bottom but couldn't. The more he thrashed the more he rose. I tried to grab hold of his outstretched hand but couldn't reach him.

The fall back position in such circumstances is to do an emergency ascent whereby you stop fighting, return to the upright position, face the surface and slowly expel all the air from your lungs. Hopefully then they won't literally explode! Thankfully Adrian remembered this and broke the surface not too worse for wear, except for dented pride and a raging heart beat.

I slowly ascended and checked that he was OK. We made our way back to the anchor chain and descended for the second time and enjoyed the dive. When we surfaced, we drank beer all the way back to the marina and related stories of our shared experience.

My ideal sport however is golf. No other sport is as brutal at tormenting the mind, nor as satisfying. Within a matter of minutes you can waver between the depths of despair and euphoric exultation. It's a rollercoaster ride that lasts hours after play has ceased. It can be just as challenging alone as in a group. It requires skill, patience, nerves of steel, concentration and cunning.

Many people don't understand the attraction. They see it only as a good walk ruined and don't see the many nuances involved. In a similar way they don't appreciate the tactics and the skill of test cricket – a 5 day game of chess. It is the ultimate contest. I'm not much of a golf watcher though and quickly tire of it when watching it on the TV.

The first time I saw a live tournament was The Australian Masters at Huntingdale and I marvelled at their distance and accuracy. I remember playing at Metropolitan and teeing off on the first par five. I played my second shot and, walking along the fairway to where my ball lay, I came across a marker which stated that this was where Greg Norman had driven his ball in the Australian Open. It was over 350 metres, and that's not all that long by today's standards. I stood on the marker and looked back at the tee in awe. What had taken me the best part of two shots had taken Norman only one.

In a golf partner you need someone who sees you for who you are and tolerates your idiosyncrasies, and I certainly had that in my favourite golf partner, Marty McKenna. We were always of the same ability and temperament and never got too down on ourselves when things weren't going our way. Marty and I played often. Both being teachers, we had time on our hands over the holidays and played at every opportunity. We had two wonderful weeks over two consecutive years camping in Eden on the New South Wales south coast where Marty and I played every day at the Merimbula and the Eden Golf Clubs. We managed to get our handicaps down to about 10, which is not too shabby if I do say so myself.

Marty is a born showman and he possesses a keen wit. His hijinks on the golf course are legendary. Once in Eden I was teeing off and oblivious to what he was up to. He had a video camera and had been filming my shots in an attempt to get under my skin. He appeared in my line of sight and coughed to attract my attention. I thought he was only asking me to smile at the camera so I was determined to ignore him. He kept persisting so I stood back and raised my eyes. There in all his glory was Marty with his pants around his ankles and still filming. I roared with laughter and that was the end of me. Marty had succeeded in breaking my concentration and won the day convincingly.

After six or seven years of surfing, golf and mis-spent summers, I returned to my old stomping ground, the Forest Hill Cricket Club. It was not however an instantly enjoyable experience and presented one of the few occasions when I have been ashamed of myself on the sporting field.

Rightly so, I was required to work my way through the grades until I reached my true level of ability. Initially I was selected in the Fifths and this sat pretty well with me. Typical of most suburban cricket clubs, the lower grades can be hard to fill and this team was short of numbers. The team was made up of a rag-tag bunch of stragglers, old timers and kids who were just keen to be chasing 5 and a half ounces of leather around the park on a Saturday afternoon.

On this occasion, I top-scored with 80-odd before fatigue and over-confidence got the better of me. As I mentioned I had a tendency to take my sport seriously and didn't necessarily differentiate between the Fifths and Firsts. It was just not in my makeup. I opened the bowling and had scored a number of scalps when a batsman skied a ball to mid off. A poor kid who had been standing in the field for hours moved to his right to take the catch and enter his name in the scorebook. A seniors' scorebook mind you, as opposed to a junior score book in which his name had probably been entered many times before. Unfortunately his moment of glory was not to be and he grassed the catch.

At this point I'd like to say that I smiled and said, 'Never mind mate, just be ready for the next one'. I would like to say that and should have said that but, regrettably, I can't and I didn't.

Instead I screamed at him, 'Fuckin' hell mate!"

I bowled the remainder of my over before the captain approached me at the change of ends.

I remember his words exactly. 'You're not in the Firsts now Pete, and he's only 14.'

I was embarrassed by my behaviour and immediately went to him and apologised profusely for my outburst. I can't help thinking though that the damage was done and maybe I was responsible for denting that kid's confidence irreparably. All those days I spent filling in for the seniors when I was as young as 14, if some big oaf had yelled at me I would have shat myself and vowed never to return.

My embarrassment and shame over this incident was heightened as I was always a tad old fashioned in my slant on sport. I believe in the old maxims that to be a sportsman, you have to look like a sportsman, act like a sportsman, and the umpire is always right. It really irked me to see a footballer with his socks down or a sportsman or woman giving both barrels to an official. I have been the butt of many jokes on the golf course regarding, as some have described, my anal approach to the contest. I have been known to take an extravagant amount of time over a shot, fully aware of how this gave my fellow players the shits, but I couldn't help that and at times quite enjoyed it. For a hack golfer some might say this is a bit rich but I believe if you're going to do anything, you may as well do it properly and to the best of your ability. And if that involves taking time over a putt, so be it.

I approached all sports in a similar way. As a cricketer I used to fashion myself on the likes of Mark Waugh, an elegant batsman who played 128 Tests for Australia. I had nowhere near his ability, but I liked his grace, his footwork and his cock-sure attitude. Whenever I came to the crease I would look like a cricketer in my pristine whites, even if I was shaking in my boots from nervousness and fear. When I bowled, I did so with purpose and intent. Even when I played 'social' netball, I prepared by shooting goals at the local primary school and implemented a shooting routine. Actually the term 'social netball' is somewhat of a misnomer because it implies friendly interaction and harmonious communion between competitors. My approach was anything but. Anal? Maybe a little.

CHAPTER 6

MY BETTER HALF – PART I

At Easter time in 1990 I spent two weeks with some friends sailing around the gorgeous Whitsunday Islands in far North Queensland. We chartered a superb 35-foot Beneteaux yacht with all the mod cons and sailed between the beautiful islands in the Whitsunday Passage, stopping off to swim in the warm waters, lie on the pure white beaches and party in the resorts dotted throughout the islands. When my fellow crew had gone to bed I would often, in various stages of inebriation, take a few minutes up on deck to lie down and listen to the halyard pinging gently against the mast and the water lapping against the hull.

One night as I gazed up to the awe-inspiring heavens, saturated by a display of light I had never seen before, my thoughts were replaced by images of a young lady who had only ten weeks prior joined Mount Lilydale College as a first year teacher. We had had some social interaction but nothing really that should suggest why in this beautiful spot and at this particularly breathtaking moment, thoughts of her would leap into my mind. Whilst thinking of her beauty, her laughter and her incredibly vivacious personality, I had a premonition that she would become a very special part of my life and that I would, in fact, marry her. It was a premonition that I had no justification for experiencing as she was in a relationship and gave no outward impression of having any interest in me whatsoever.

It is funny but I had had such premonitions before when I would experience a feeling of unqualified clarity and conviction about something. The first occurred during my Higher School Certificate (HSC), just prior to exams. I was walking near my home and was stopped in my tracks by a thought that had entered my consciousness. Actually it was not so much a thought but an aura that enveloped me and I knew with absolute certainty that I would do well in my exams. The feeling was palpable and stimulated all of my senses.

The second such experience was equally as tangible. I was surfing with my mate Kevin Logan who had just caught a wave and I found myself alone sitting on my board at the back of the line-up. The conditions were perfect with a good swell and a slight offshore breeze blowing the spray from the breaking waves gently back into my face. The swell temporarily abated and I was becalmed, sitting in pure and perfect silence when suddenly an extraordinary repose came over me.

Time became suspended and I had an acute sense that I was not alone. I remain convinced that I witnessed, there and then, the actual presence of God.

Now, I am not a particularly religious man and don't make a habit of encountering manifestations of the Holy Spirit, but I am sure that I experienced some sort of divine closeness. I felt warmth within and was at one with the world. Again, the feeling was palpable and as real as the board beneath me, the icy water and the cloudless sky.

At the moment I lay on deck glaring at the stars above, having been struck by the power of my premonition, I determined that I would not die wondering and would upon my return to school subtly make a play for Lee's affection.

Early in the second term a few of the younger members of staff decided to institute a social committee, as morale had been waning and there was a distinct lack of opportunities for such a large staff to socialise on any organised level. I saw this as my moment to be proactive in my play for Lee as she had signalled her intention to become involved in the committee. I don't know who I thought I was kidding, but before long all my closest friends on staff caught on that I was keen and began their clandestine activities on my behalf - without, I might add, my permission. Were my feelings reciprocated? How seriously was she involved with her boyfriend? Et cetera, et cetera. Believe me when I say I needed all the help I could get.

The committee started working on our first big gig – a cocktail party to be held at semester's end. A week prior to the party, one of my undercover operatives (though probably a double agent) excitedly approached me saying that Lee had recently broken it off with her boyfriend and would be amenable to an advance from me.

I summoned all the courage I could muster and approached her, quite stupidly and unprofessionally, while she was supervising 200 screaming Year 7s on yard duty.

'Hey Lee,' I said as nonchalantly as I could with my teeth chattering and knees buckling, 'Would you like to grab a bite to eat next Saturday night, just you and me?'

She smiled distractedly.

'Sorry, Pete, I'd like to but I've actually got other plans on Saturday.'

As always Lee was polite, friendly and to the point. But she didn't appear particularly flattered nor did she expand on what her other plans were.

Not wanting to lose all self-respect I replied, 'Oh it's no big deal, maybe some other time.'

With that I engaged in some small talk, bid her adieu and made a hasty retreat around the corner where I beat myself about the head and chastised myself for being so stupid. I felt shattered and silly, had obviously misread the signs, and had relied on flawed intelligence. I immediately became resigned to the fact this liaison was just not meant to be. Yes, I ashamedly admit that with one knock-back I was going to quit. That is the sum of the man, or wimp, I was.

The following Friday evening the cocktail party was in full swing and it became evident that we needed more ice. I volunteered to walk to the 7 Eleven nearby and Mary Craven, a friend and colleague, volunteered Lee to help.

'You two might have something to talk about,' she said.

I had no idea what she meant and was still smarting over the events earlier in the week. But I went with Lee anyway and as we walked, Lee said casually that her plans for Saturday had fallen through.

'If the offer still stands, I'd like to have dinner with you,' she said shyly.

Well, my heart leapt and I could hardly contain my excitement. It is the best party I have ever been to and as I departed, Lee and I kissed as the sun dawned to greet the new, glorious day.

The next evening Lee and I had the date I had so pathetically asked her about the week before. As she climbed into my car, a very drafty Volkswagen Beetle convertible, I reached into the back seat and extracted a sizeable bunch of flowers, the first of many I would shower her with over the years. We should have been tired given that we had no sleep the night before but we had a truly fantastic evening and were completely at ease in each other's company. We laughed as if there was no tomorrow and to me it just felt right.

The following six months were very exciting as we threw ourselves headlong into our new relationship, leaving notes on each other's desk and spending every free moment in each other's company. But for a few close friends we tried to keep our relationship from the rest of the staff and school community for two reasons. Firstly, we wanted to conduct ourselves purely on a professional level whilst at work. Both of us took our work seriously and were fearful of not being seen in this light if news of our relationship became public property.

Secondly, at the same time as our love was developing, I just so happened to be teaching Lee's sister Melissa in Year 12 Legal Studies. She was one of my finest students, completely dedicated, conscientious and bright. Both Lee and I did not want to place her in a difficult position by rendering her susceptible to unfair accusations of favouritism or make life in any way uncomfortable for her. Our fears, as it turned out were, in fact, warranted because as rumours of our liaison spread through the College community she was subjected to a few barbs from disgruntled and jealous classmates and friends. It was a minefield for the two of us and I had to tread very carefully in order to minimise the social fallout for Melissa and the academic impact of me being her teacher in such a crucial year. To her credit and certainly none of my own, she was dux of my class and was the recipient of the Departmental Award for Excellence.

The following year, news of our relationship became widely known and indeed celebrated. Yet I began to get annoyed at the intrusion into our personal lives and the claustrophobic nature of our partnership. I was struggling and confused by seeing Lee every day at work and having to act as if we were just colleagues. Sometimes she was stressed or just having a bad day but I perceived this to be acting coldly or angrily toward me. I would then get my back up or worry that I had done something wrong. Or worse, maybe she was having second thoughts about our relationship! I was consumed by my own insecurities and inadequacies and was tiring of it. We spent all our free time together and shared every aspect of our professional lives.

I remember driving to the beach one weekend and having nothing to say in the car on the way. We simply had every aspect of our lives in common.

CHAPTER 7

MOVING ON

THROUGHOUT 1991 I became increasingly dissatisfied with working at Mount Lilydale. Mainly because of my blossoming relationship with Lee but also because this was the only school I had experienced and if I was to become a serious player in the world of education I had to broaden my horizons. However, this was not an easy decision to make as I loved everything about Mount Lilydale – the staff, the kids and their families, even the grounds and the view over the Yarra Valley. I can still remember as if it were yesterday the sweet smell of jasmine and the crisp air as I strode to my car for the last time in the knowledge that one day I'd be back.

At the end of 1991 I applied for, and was successful in attaining, a position as Dormitory Supervisor at Assumption College, Kilmore, about 60 kilometres north of Melbourne. This role primarily involved me taking responsibility for the Year 10 dormitory that housed

35 boys. Picture a large room containing bunks with cupboards at the foot of each bed in which the boarders kept all their worldly possessions. At one end of the dorm was my office through which was my sleeping quarters, containing a bed, shower and toilet.

My day started at 6am. After showering and dressing I would hit the radio button in response to which there'd be a stampede for the showers. Being at altitude, the climate was much like that of Ballarat with freezing mornings and, once out of bed, the boys were not prone to standing around chatting. After all the boys were showered and dressed in their uniforms, we'd head downstairs to the 'ref' for breakfast. Afterwards we would return to the dorm, clean up, make all beds, vacuum and then be 'released' into the wider school community. On the odd occasion I'd need to send a kid who was not well enough to attend school to the infirmary.

I was first port of call if the day school required a replacement teacher and eight days out of 10 this was the case. I'd lock the dorm, rush over to the staffroom and find out my allocation of classes, which invariably was a full day's teaching. At the completion of the school day I needed to be back in the dorm to open up for the return of the boarders so that they could change for sports training. All boarders were required to be engaged in some form of sporting team and most needed no convincing. Many, in fact, were at Assumption for precisely that reason, as the school had a formidable reputation on the sporting arena – especially Australian Rules football and cricket. Many were of country origin, coming from as far as Queensland, but a few also came from the city to get expert football coaching.

I was a cricket coach and so had to get myself changed and be in the nets by 4pm during the cricket season. After training we'd open the showers and be ready for dinner by 6pm. Dinner was a challenging time with 175 testosterone-charged young men, fresh off the training track with ravenous appetites, lining up to be fed. Thankfully I was only on ref duty twice a week and was usually able to eat in the more salubrious surroundings of the Marist Brothers dining room where digestion was far easier.

After dishes were stacked and tables wiped, the boys could catch up on some television before heading off to study hall. My guys had to do 1 and a half hours per night. I had the task of supervising all the boarders in partnership with Brother Doug, the Dormitory Master, a stern but caring man who exercised firm discipline with the boys. The young ones feared him but as they came to know him the relationship grew into one of admiration and respect. As the year progressed he placed increasing responsibility for the operation of the boarding school into my hands. The boys were expected to study in silence and this expectation was strictly enforced. After study they headed to the ref for a snack, back to the dorm for free time before lights-out at 10.45.

This was undoubtedly the most difficult time of the day in my job. Some of the more challenging students found it hard to entertain themselves and prowled the dorm looking for trouble, usually at the expense of the weaker boys. Early in the year I had a hard time nullifying their influence but was determined to do so. Interestingly, these boys were new to the boarding school, sent for precisely the reason that we were now witnessing; they were either not welcome anywhere else, or their parents were at their wits end and saw the regimen, order and discipline of boarding school as the answer. Some of these new boys initially found the routine hard to cope with and regularly pushed the boundaries of acceptable conduct. Unfortunately for them, there is no place to hide in boarding life and no shortage of tasks that need doing. If they were going to misuse their free time, then I had plenty up my sleeve to keep them busy.

Boarding life was difficult for some. Even the most experienced ones had down moments and missed their families awfully. The physical set-up of the dorm did not help as it provided absolutely no privacy. You could not dress, shower, sleep, or sit on your bed and read without being under the watchful eye of 35 others. There was rarely a quiet corner in which to retreat and everything the individual owned was public property. To hoard one's own belongings was inviting scorn and derision from the rest. A boarder could not open his 'press' (the cupboard at the end of his bed) without having inquisitive eyes cast over his shoulder to see what loot was stored within. Some boys, after returning from a holiday at home, were notorious for bringing back to the dorm all manner of fare and used it as currency to trade favours like getting out of ref duty or morning clean-up. It was common to see boarders return after holidays with bags stuffed full with two-minute noodles, the legal tender of the dorm. Those who were smart rationed theirs until late term when noodles were scarce and market forces drove up their wealth and, hence, their power.

I worked very hard in my dorm to counter the two or three bullies and standover merchants by creating a cooperative, friendly and respectful atmosphere. For some, this behaviour was more an aberration and some counselling, encouragement and positive reinforcement was effective in helping them realise the harm they were causing. Often when kids are taught to step out of their egocentricity and empathise with others they begin to get a new perspective of the world and their place within it. For others more punitive measures were adopted and, in one case, eventual expulsion from the boarding school was the only option.

It is not enough, however, to simply deal with those who make life difficult for others. Often one needs to address with the 'victim' certain aspects of their behaviour that sees them singled out. This should in no way be viewed as shifting the blame from the perpetrator to the bullied – everyone has the right to feel safe and one must always tackle the issue from this starting point. However, as I found myself in a quasi-parental role, I believed it was incumbent on me to empower these kids with skills to deflect the barbs sent their way and coach them towards attending to certain reactive and abrasive aspects of their own personality. It was their desire to learn how to be accepted, to fit in and feel like a part of the community. It was not a matter of changing personalities but, more-over, helping them adapt to the circumstances they found themselves in by learning how to negotiate, cooperate and compromise.

Most boys derived many positives out of the boarding experience, as did I. The sense of collegiality and group spirit they realised from the year was obvious and, if the feedback from their parents was any indication, I was pleased with my efforts. I developed an attachment and respect for the boarders for theirs was a tough existence compared to most others their age. Rarely did they bellyache about the cold, uncomfortable conditions or when being hauled out of bed at 5am to fill in for a team playing on the Mornington Peninsula when a day-school student had failed to show, or when cleaning and maintaining the college grounds for which other people were paid. These days if you so much as suggest that a student pick up his or her own rubbish you might get a face-full of attitude about the role of the cleaning staff. We shared many laughs and celebrated milestones together – we were family.

Early on in the year though, I knew that my days in this caper were numbered. Eighteen-hour days and working two weekends in three was not my idea of a career and I sorely missed Lee and my family and friends.

I don't automatically know why I took on the job in the first place. With the aid of hindsight I guess I was testing the strength of the bond Lee and I shared and our ability to withstand adversity. We spoke on the telephone every day but missed each other terribly and at the end of 1992 I gladly returned to Melbourne to take on a new role and assume some normality in our relationship. I was pleased we had not only withstood the test but our love had developed to the point where we were comfortable being apart. I believe this came to be one of the strengths of our relationship in that we never needed to be in the other's pocket. We led separate lives and were quite happy doing so, but at the end of the day enjoyed sharing our different experiences, outlooks and ideas.

CHAPTER 8

ONWARDS AND UPWARDS

IN JANUARY 1993 I began the role of Assistant to the Deputy Principal and Assistant Religious Education Co-ordinator at Salesian College in Chadstone. The Religious Education Coordinator role was very 'un-me' and I initially struggled. This role involved leading the very robust liturgy program of six masses every week, in which I had to play my guitar and 'encourage' 200 boys to sing along with me to old hymns. Needless to say this was like extracting teeth and more often than not I was the only one singing. If it meant being closer to Lee, though, then I was up for it and willing to give anything a go.

In my role I began working closely with Salesian's then Deputy Principal, Michael Scott, who was a very wise and gentle soul and he taught me a great deal. In partnership we worked hard at making drastic changes to the curriculum and turned the liturgical program over to the Religious Education teachers and their students, making for a far more meaningful liturgical experience.

Unfortunately it had become evident to the two of us that one area in which the school was sorely lacking was student welfare. There was no one person responsible for overseeing a comprehensive and coordinated student welfare program. My role seemed the best fit for such a function but I was not formally qualified to tackle such a monumental task. In 1994 I therefore embarked on further study at Melbourne University, undertaking a Graduate Diploma in Student Welfare over two years.

As it turned out, however, upon completing my studies I managed to score a role as Year 9 Co-ordinator, which was far more to my liking and better suited my skills. This role involved being responsible for the welfare of 165 Year 9 boys, some aspects of the curriculum and the staff who taught them.

The main function of a Coordinator at this level is one of discipline. This is unfortunate because there were so many other worthwhile ways for me to spend my time in more strategic pursuits such as curriculum design, behavioural management programs and teacher support. There were moments when I sat in my office and cringed at the person I had become and the way I had just behaved towards an individual, group or even the whole level. Sometimes I had to address behavioural issues with an iron fist, not because that was the best way to deal with them, but for expediency; there are only so many hours in the day and with the number of issues that arose, there seemed little time for individual counselling. I learnt much about myself during this time, mainly about my ability to cope under intense stress but also my ability to really connect with kids from diverse backgrounds, to listen and not presume that I understood where they were coming from, and to never, ever judge them based on their behaviour.

There are many and varied reasons why kids behave as they do. I learnt to deal with the behaviour on the one hand but also try to understand the reasons for it. This was far easier to do as a Coordinator because I was emotionally detached from the student's initial behaviour. Usually I had to deal with issues that had been referred to me by a class teacher. When you begin to delve below the surface, you get a much clearer understanding of the motivating factors.

I remember one boy, a very clever kid who was always being sent to my office for destroying his classes. He had chewed up and spat out a few teachers in his time at the college but had managed to make it into Year 9. I'd had a gutful of him and was receiving little support from his parents. I determined that this had to stop or his enrolment at the college would be under review.

I called a final meeting with his parents to discuss my views but, again, as was customary, only his mother arrived. During the meeting I brutally laid the cards on the table and asked if he would like a final word. To that, he and his mother broke down and explained that his father was battling severe schizophrenia and the student was fearful that he too was beginning to show signs of the disease. In an instant I saw all of his previous misbehaviour in a completely different light. I had assumed so much about this poor kid without realising how much his destructive behaviour was motivated by something else – his terrible fear and incredibly difficult home life. I was chastened but grateful for the timely wake-up call, as from that point on we had planned intervention and family support and his behaviour improved markedly. As for me, I became wary from then on about making judgment based solely on poor behaviour.

By far the most challenging aspect of coordinating a year level is staff relations. Often teachers became infuriated by the behaviour of a student or even that of an entire class and sought immediate relief by demanding my presence. While usually justified, on the odd occasion the teacher had over-stepped the mark and was reacting to a situation that was, in fact, due to his or her own making. There were other occasions where teachers simply weren't up to the task of teaching. We all knew who they were and the kids saw them coming a mile off but unfortunately they had now become my problem and needed to be skilled-up post haste. This was a tall order given that some had been in the system for over 20 years. It took all of my skill and nerve to approach such people but they often responded positively and worked hard to adopt my suggestions.

I was never one to dress down a colleague as it was not in my make-up, but if I became frustrated by numerous months of incompetence and their stubbornness against at least attempting change, then they lost my support and I would simply intercede on the kids' behalf. It perplexes me why a person, and I have encountered them in every school I have been associated with, would enter a profession to which they are so unsuited that they have nothing positive to say and actually give the impression of disliking kids. We all know the type – the moaners, whingers and complainers who add nothing to the organisation but misery and put road blocks in the way of new ideas, innovation and change. I pity them for it must be a terribly long drive to work and the daily grind so monotonous and banal that it could be likened to water torture. I could not think of anything worse than having no intensity or passion for what I was doing.

Perhaps the most valuable thing I learned from my time at Salesian was their approach to the kids in their care. The Salesian religious order was founded by Saint John Bosco who worked amongst disadvantaged youth in the ghettos of Turin in Italy during the 19th century. He wrote about the need to love the kids in your care and to let them know they are loved. He spoke about being 'with' the kids, getting amongst them and befriending them. This was very much the focus at Salesian College and characterised the starting point in relations between staff and students – we called it 'Salesianity'. It was commonplace to see teachers out at lunchtime involved in games with the kids or having a kick of the footy on the oval. I fondly remember Brother Joe, Brother Steve and Brother Martin who did not teach at the college but came over from the residence during the lunch break to be with the kids. In my time at the school we persevered with many students that others would have given up on. Of course, the old adage about leading a horse to water is also true and when a kid's behaviour became such that it was continually and severely impacting on others, we would reluctantly adopt the hard edge of Salesianity and move the student on.

Undoubtedly the aspect of the role I disliked most was public speaking. Unfortunately this came with the territory and on numerous occasions a year, I would have to address large gatherings of parents at curriculum evenings and information sessions. It is strange that I could speak to 1000 students without batting an eyelid but the prospect of 400 adults gave me sleepless nights. I prepared thoroughly, writing copious notes and would rehearse over and over again. Even at staff meetings where I was driving the agenda I was nervous, but certainly gave little or no indication of being so. Colleagues used to comment on how cool and calm I was when addressing large groups but my composed and placid exterior belied that underneath I was paddling like hell just to remain afloat. Instead of becoming more relaxed as I became accustomed to addressing large groups, I actually grew increasingly tense.

I remain convinced that I showed the signs of MND as early as 1996 because the shaking and queasiness became worse from that point. In late 2000 when I departed Salesian College and nine months before I was diagnosed, I made a farewell speech and was so nervous I couldn't keep my right leg from jerking up and down and my voice from audibly quivering.

CHAPTER 9

THE HAPPIEST DAY OF MY LIFE

THE DAY LEE and I were married - Easter Sunday in 1995 – was the happiest day of my life. I toiled for a long time over penning the words for this chapter, and for good reason; I simply didn't know how to do the day justice.

It was a stormy day and the sky threatened rain all day. I will never forget how radiant Lee looked and how confident she was as she advanced down the aisle, even though she'd had to wait ten minutes in the foyer while our best man frantically tried to get the Forrest Gump Suite to play!

I, on the other hand, was a mess as I articulated my vows timidly in front of all those present. Again, I was not used to all the attention being focussed on me. Some of my friends were put off by my shakiness but I was just flustered by all the attention of the hundred odd guests waiting in the church. Lee was superb, however, and all I needed was to look into her eyes for grounding.

'Leanne, I ask you to share my life, to be my wife, best friend and partner.

I promise you my loyalty, respect and honesty.

May we share our experiences with patience, thoughtfulness and understanding.

I will love, cherish and care for you, for the rest of my life.'

I will attest to being somewhat chuffed that - of all her suitors - Lee had in fact chosen to marry me.

We had a bridal party of one each; Mark Evans was my best man and Lee's younger sister, Melissa, was the Maid of Honour. Fittingly, Year 7 students from Mount Lilydale College were ushers for the ceremony, and the school's former chaplain, Father Michael Elligate, was our celebrant.

For our photos we went down to St Kilda Beach before setting off to Churches in Richmond for our cocktail reception. Marty McKenna played music on Churches' grand piano as our guests entered and then we danced the night away to our mate Brendan Douglas' band. The traditional speeches ranged from the sentimental to the silly and tears of joy and laughter flowed as Lee and I spoke, Mark Evans performed a memorable puppet show and my father-in-law Kevin toasted us warmly.

A romantic honeymoon night at the stately Windsor hotel capped off our special day. The following morning we boarded a plane and headed up to Noosa for our honeymoon. Once again I was in Queensland, five years since I sailed the waters and had a premonition in the dead of night about a first year teacher at Mount Lilydale. That first year teacher was now Leanne Anderson, my beautiful wife.

CHAPTER 10

THE EARLY SIGNS

NEWLY MARRIED, I could not have been happier with my life outside the classroom. However, at work, I had started to become disillusioned in my role as a teacher. It was a very gradual feeling of disenchantment brought on by long hours, high stress and lack of remuneration. I also perceived a lack of regard in the population for teachers generally and over a long period began to devalue my own worth. I just didn't feel that I was contributing or producing anything of significance and this outlook began to erode my enjoyment of doing the job. I guess in all the stress I started losing sight of who I was and why I became a teacher in the first place. The bright-eyed sponge was becoming parched and I started dwelling on the negative aspects of the job.

Not wanting to join the ranks of the whingers I quickly adopted a proactive approach and began to look beyond teaching. I analysed the skills and interests I possessed which were transferable to the business environment and in 1998 again found myself at university studying a Graduate Diploma of Human Resources.

It was very gruelling studying part-time and working in a demanding job but I managed to successfully juggle the two over the next two years. It was also difficult to keep performing in my work whilst looking outside for other opportunities. I actually felt like a traitor coming to work and sending off emails to headhunters and recruiters. Thankfully, coordinating my Year 9s still provided enough challenges to keep me keen and very, very busy and my election as the administration team's representative on the Board gave me added incentive to keep ploughing ahead.

Sport also continued to play a part in motivating me outside the classroom. In 1998, Leanne and I were invited to join a mixed netball team in a local competition. I jumped at the chance to involve myself again in a team environment and it seemed like a good way for Lee and I to keep fit together. I grew to love the game of netball and became quite a useful Goal Attack and Goal Shooter. Before long I also became involved in my brother-in-law Mark's team and found myself playing twice a week. Netball requires much more strategy and entails every member of the team becoming involved because play is more positional and the ball must be transferred through the three sections of the court. As it transpired, Lee and I took over the management of the team and before long it constituted all of our closest friends and family. Thursday nights became a much anticipated time of the week and though there was much jocularity on court, there was no mistaking that we were playing for keeps. Over two years we played off in a number of finals but never cracked it for a win.

At the same time I also began running. I had at previous stages in my adulthood attempted to run distances but was never capable of maintaining the required discipline. I would always start out with the best of intentions but the monotony, boredom and pain thwarted any sustained effort. Mark, my brother who was living in Sydney, was preparing to run the Sydney Marathon over the same course as the approaching 2000 Olympic Games. His hard work and dedication inspired me and I began to hold notions of one day running alongside him. As I had never been a runner it was imperative that I start slowly over short distances and build up a fitness base to work from. Before too long I was up around the five-six kilometre range and doing some pretty good times. I don't really know what was different this time around but I managed to persevere through the hard slog of those early months when I would slow to a walk after no more than a kilometre with an excruciating stitch in my side.

After a few months I found myself looking forward to returning home from work, pulling on my running gear and hitting the pavement. I actually became quite obsessive about it and would plan my route during the day and set goals along the way. In hindsight, my work was also very stressful at the time and running provided me the opportunity to leave it all behind and process a lot of information in my head. By the time I returned home in a lather of perspiration I was completely relaxed and totally at ease with the world.

In 1999, after four or five months of running, I began to notice that I was not recovering very well after a run, particularly in my right calf. This did seem unusual because by this stage I expected to be a great deal more flexible than I was. The rest of my body was fine but my right leg was playing tricks. I also noticed that as I came to critical fatigue moments on my run I could not stride out as far with my right leg as I could with my left. There was only a very subtle change, but a noticeable one none the less. It was at this stage I also found that I was sore through my right groin and lower abdomen. Just a slight soreness, but enough to hamper my efforts when running and playing netball. I felt sure that I was displaying the classic symptoms of a hernia and finally sought the advice of a doctor.

The doctor gave me a clean bill of health, suggesting that maybe I was pushing myself too hard and that I should modify my routine. I took his advice but after a short time the symptoms returned. A work colleague suggested I see a specialist in the area of sports medicine and he provided me with the necessary details.

I remember vividly how intimidated I felt sitting in the doctor's waiting room with walls adorned by signed photographs of Australia's leading sportsmen and women singing the praises of this particular physician. My consultation left me no less intimidated and inferior as he cast an eye over my puny body saying that my legs were "underdeveloped", to which a friend later remarked that perhaps his standards were somewhat higher than most. The sports physician subsequently sent me to see a similarly intimidating physiotherapist for an X-ray, the results of which suggested nothing conclusive save some wear and tear of the hip joint from my cricket days.

In the meantime I continued with my physical activity though had cut back my netball to one night a week. I was still experiencing discomfort after running, as well as some acute pain in the testicles, which turned out to be an abscess, or pilonidal cyst, that had been dormant for quite a while but had become infected due to my increased sporting activity. The doctor was doubtful that this was the cause of my presenting problems, as was I, but he felt the need to address this issue none the less. I was immediately referred to a colo-rectal surgeon who treated the cyst with antibiotics and, after the infection had cleared, a day surgery procedure was performed to remove the cyst.

However the healing progress was far too slow and, after three months, the surgeon expressed concern that without scraping the scar tissue out the wound, it would take even longer. Again I had to front up for surgery but this time the outcome was far more positive.

Eventually the wound healed over, just in time for Lee and I to jet off to Thailand for a much-needed break. The months of frustrating rehabilitation, as well as the emotions of my father's death earlier that year, had taken a toll.

Within weeks of our return I was back running, but as soon as I pushed myself, it was clear that my muscular problems had progressed and I became somewhat concerned.

I was back on the medical merry-go-round but this time went to a different GP, one Lee had recommended. He had been her family doctor for some years, and expressed some concern at my symptoms, immediately referring me to a neurologist. Even at this stage there was no obvious sign of anything particularly sinister. I walked with a normal gait, my speech was fine and I felt very fit. It was only when I exerted myself that I began to suffer any sign of physical abnormality; the dragging right leg, the ache in my calf, the soreness in my right groin and lower abdomen.

The neurologist put me through a number of preliminary tests, mainly to analyse my reflexes and muscle strength. It became obvious that my reflexes were on edge in my right leg and there was some atrophy in the muscles. After nearly a year of blood tests, MRI and CAT scans, and a barrage of other diagnostic tests, I was still none the wiser as to what was causing my symptoms.

One of the myriad of tests conducted was an electromyography (EMG). This involves inserting a long needle connected by wires to a machine into major muscles to monitor the electrical activity under the skin that may be otherwise invisible to the naked eye. I can assure you that these tests, conducted over a number of weeks, are very unpleasant and in the end still came up inconclusive.

During the testing, which took place over almost ten months, there had been no mention of any particular condition or disease. In fact, there seemed to be very little change in my physical condition, so I didn't seek further medical intervention for another few months as there seemed little point.

Similarly, my doctor decided to take a wait-and-see approach to determine if there was any progression in my condition over time.

CHAPTER 11

THE BIRTH OF ELIZA

AMONGST ALL OF this concern and anxiety with my testing, Lee and I were blessed with the greatest gift of all – the birth of our daughter, Eliza.

On 21 May 2000, Lee was rushed to Mitcham Private Hospital for an emergency caesarean section. When we arrived at the hospital we waited for more than four hours as the foetal monitor dipped from 135 beats per minute down to as low as 78. With the midwives growing increasingly concerned, it was with great relief when the obstetrician finally arrived and took charge, ordering a caesarean immediately.

Time was a blur and I cannot remember how long later Eliza May arrived, a scrawny baby girl 51 centimetres tall and weighing 3004 grams. While Lee was recovering from her surgery I got my first of many beautiful photos with my most treasured possession.

That photo took pride of place in Eliza's baby album,

along with other significant papers and milestones from her baby days. One such significant piece of paper is the thank you letter I wrote on Eliza's behalf, to all her family and friends who had welcomed her so warmly, and supported Lee and I so well, in those first few months.

It read:

"Mum and Dad said I should write to all our family and friends who demonstrated such overwhelming kindness and generosity when I was born.

I'm only a few weeks old and already I have such wonderful friends to play with. I'm getting to know Mum and Dad a bit too. They seem OK, although I can't get a decent night's sleep because Mum's always cleaning my room and Dad keeps peering into my cradle to wake me. It's great fun watching them scurry around tending to my every desire. All I have to do is cry! I suppose they were a bit shaken up by my arrival.

My life has so far been fairly non-eventful. I wake up, have a drink, poo my pants, have another drink, poo my pants again, lie in my rocker, and then go to sleep (even then I can still poo my pants.)

I really hope that we get to see a lot of each other in the future. Thank you so much for all you have done for me and for Mum and Dad.

With much love,

Eliza."

From the outset, I nicknamed Eliza 'Lizey Lou', a name that holds to this day. The childhood bedtime classics also became favourites between us, most notably "It's Time for Bed" and "Guess How Much I Love You".

I was, and still am, totally besotted with my daughter.

I returned to work at Salesian as proud as I have ever been. It was no longer just Lee and I, we had a family of our own and we were determined to cherish every moment of our new life.

Four months later we took our first family holiday together, taking Eliza on her first of many trips to Queensland. The trip also doubled as a break ahead of the beginning of my new career, as after hundreds of applications and a few interviews I had landed the very lofty position of Business Consultant with a firm in St Kilda Road, Melbourne.

Upon returning from Queensland I left Salesian College, which was not easy. I departed with many good friends, fond memories and that special 'Salesian Spirit' which, in hindsight, was probably the reason I found my next move so unsatisfying.

CHAPTER 12

A MOMENTARY AFFLICTION

THE FIRM I started with in 2000 was the third largest business consultancy in Europe, had expanded into Sydney and was just starting to establish a presence in Melbourne. Lee and I were wined and dined by the Managing Director who placed a very attractive package before me the following day.

I joined a small team in the Melbourne office of five consultants and two support staff. Our role was to provide a range of business services, mainly recruitment, management development and organisational development tools to companies throughout Australia and the Asia-Pacific region. Of course, before we could provide the services, we had to sell them and this involved cold-calling at least 30-40 businesses a week, through which you might get four or five meetings, out of which may come one client. In my first two months I was not expected to make sales calls but simply follow one of the more seasoned guys to meetings and provide support.

After the first few months I began to find that this consulting game was not rocket science. I removed my rose coloured glasses and began to take a more discerning view of what was happening around me as well as most importantly the underlying values of the organisation. I had developed in the pit of my stomach a knot that wouldn't go away —an uneasiness, the cause of which I couldn't put my finger on.

Initially I put it down to the nervous tension of being so far outside of my comfort zone and embarking on the great unknown of a new career. However, it was becoming increasingly evident that I just didn't fit this environment and didn't espouse the same values. Nor did I share things in common with my colleagues, who were very competitive, hardcore sales types and jealously guarded their own methods, approaches and techniques. I was a babe in the woods and - given very little opportunity to learn from them - I felt very much out in the cold. I could cope with this and would have, in time, developed my own strategies. What I couldn't abide was the callous approach to the 'sell' and the manner in which clients or job applicants were treated.

Outwardly the company touted its ethical standards. However, I witnessed countless examples of people taking short cuts and, considerably worse, episodes of sexism, racism and bullying. Sri Lankans were referred to as 'tea pickers' with the commonly held belief that persons of this ethnic group did not make good employees and embellished their qualifications. As soon as a person of that race entered for an interview, the code 'M5' would be scrawled on their résumé, indicating that the support staff should automatically send a 'thanks, but no thanks' letter.

The Managing Director was an autocrat who thought nothing of bailing up a consultant and aggressively bawling him or her out like a naughty child. I was on the receiving end of a couple of abusive episodes and remain ashamed of myself for being so submissive in the face of his unfair criticisms and the obscene manner in which they were communicated. I suppose I was used to a workplace where people pulled together and had more altruistic motives for being there. Perhaps I was naive and just too soft for this business environment, but I couldn't work under these conditions.

After six months of telling myself it would all be okay, I became resigned to the fact that this organisation was not for me. The last straw came when, on the way to work early one morning in March 2001, a motorist came straight through a red light, T-boned my car and sent me spinning into oncoming traffic.

My brand new car was as good as a write-off.

Shaken and sore and in the hands of an ambulance crew, I rang the office to inform them of my accident and that I could not come in. Not a single person rang me at home to check on my condition and nobody thought to inform the Managing Director. Upon my return to work none of my colleagues felt the need to inquire about my welfare.

Until this point I had kept my doubts from Lee, but now I had to broach the issue and explain my extreme anxiety and the unhappiness eating away at my gut. Unfortunately, deep down I felt like a complete failure for not being able to tough this period out. But it was just not in me to go through the motions until something better came along.

Lee would have none of this defeatist talk and applied her usual calmness and wisdom to my predicament.

'You can't be in a workplace like that Pete,' she said simply.

'Do something about it, make a change – you don't have to put up with that crap.'

I learned that my work was more to me than simply a job or a means to an end. It must have greater meaning than status or money. I needed connectivity to my workplace and my colleagues, a sense that we were all working towards some common goal or vision and in so doing we looked out for and respected one another. I yearned for a more profound significance to my labour – a purpose and meaning beyond the dollar and one's own self-interest. In short, I realised that the environment in which I thrived was, in fact, the one I had just left.

The next day I contacted the MD in Sydney and resigned – effective immediately.

That night I rang all of my contacts at various schools around town and the offers came thick and fast for replacement work until I decided what I would do in the long term. I am proud of the fact that I only had one day off between leaving the consulting firm and taking up the various teaching jobs. Michael Scott, with whom I had worked at Salesian and was now working at Mount Lilydale Mercy College, suggested that I consider returning to Mount Lilydale to replace the Year 12 Coordinator, who was taking long service leave.

I duly met with the Principal, Bernard Dobson, who offered me the position. The role was initially only for a term but I was led to believe that with various reshuffles taking place over the remainder of the year, I would be in the role for the longer term. Bernard was also keen for me to bring to the college some of my human resource management expertise, which further sweetened the deal.

So there I was back at Mount Lilydale. My professional life had come full circle.

There was something poetic in the fact that here, in the place where I started my career, I would also end it.

CHAPTER 13

BACK TO THE BEGINNING

I TOOK TO my new role like a duck to water. I had 220 17-18-year-old girls and boys in my charge and I loved every minute of it. It was very hard work and I had to hit the ground running. Nevertheless, I was incredibly well-supported, in particular by the previous Year 12 Coordinator, Dianne De Munk, the Head of Senior School, Michael Johnston, and Mount Lilydale's Deputy Principal, Mark Prest. In fact all the staff, especially the Year 12 team, seemed to gauge that it was a tall order to come in at such a time and did their utmost to make the transition easier for me – such a contrast from my experience in the business consultancy.

Year 12 presents many challenges for students, most of whom are ably equipped to suffer them. Some, however, struggle on various levels to meet the rigours of the year and the expectations of a largely caring, vastly experienced and understanding staff. Most of my time was spent with these students, counselling them, chatting to them, meeting with their parents and, sometimes, disciplining them. My previous experience at coordinating a year level involved far more coercion than the Year 12s required, making this a profoundly more fulfilling experience.

The legacy of the Salesian spirit had also affected me greatly and I took it with me into this role. It was my goal to spend at least 15 minutes every lunchtime moving amongst the kids, chatting informally and keeping my ear to the ground. That's not to say I didn't need to crack the whip every now and then or that my patience wasn't sorely tested. Students wouldn't be students if they didn't test the boundaries once in a while and I had my fair share of run-ins. Interestingly, these were most prevalent when their teachers were ramping up the workload or a number of SACs (School Assessed Coursework) were due.

I immediately found that the nature of the students' issues I was dealing with was complex and 'adult'. To all intents and purposes these 'kids' were adults and demanded to be treated as such. Many drove cars, paid taxes, were sexually active, drank to excess, and a couple lived away from home. The problem is that many people of this age lack the emotional maturity and the life experience to cope with the subtext of being an adult. I guess many adults do too. They had, to varying degrees, outgrown the institution, its rules and its regimen, and my modus operandi was to strike the balance. Basically I had to trust them and let them know they were trusted. Every student began with a clean slate and if anyone slipped up they received the benefit of the doubt. The student body largely responded to this approach and I was pleased with the tone in the Year 12 corridor and the manner in which they were responding to me. I began to develop a genuine affection towards them, was keen for them to do well, and was disappointed when individuals or groups let me down.

A little over two months after I took on the job, came the fateful evening of 21 June 2001, when my world came crashing down.

CHAPTER 14

THE DIAGNOSIS

EARLIER IN JUNE 2001, Lee and I went out with close friends Fiona and Nick Deed to dinner at Indochine, which was our favourite Vietnamese restaurant in Box Hill. We were set for a fun night with good friends, great food and a few drinks. However, as the evening progressed, I began to feel terribly affected by the alcohol I had consumed. (Mind you, I only had two stubbies of beer over a couple of hours, much less than I could normally tolerate.) In particular, my right leg became very stiff and I had some trouble walking. My speech also became noticeably slurred and I was quite embarrassed by my obvious drunkenness. I remember walking to the car feeling quite distressed at my condition. I made the decision to make an appointment with the neurologist first thing Monday morning.

When Lee and I fronted up to the neurologist, I was somewhat nervous because, in the preceding week, I had researched my symptoms on the internet. Medical professionals the world over have termed this phenomenon 'cyberchondria' – people armed with a computer, but little or no medical knowledge, tend to misdiagnose themselves and present to their GPs having completely misread their symptoms. I managed to convince myself that my symptoms were characteristic of someone suffering from multiple sclerosis. Even so, I was sure that such a diagnosis would be some way off after months of further testing and consultation with numerous specialists. I was confident that my meeting with the neurologist would lead me no closer to an outcome. That just seemed to be the way of the medical merry-go-round I had found myself riding.

I guess in hindsight Lee had also been frightened by my level of impairment at the restaurant, as she had rarely accompanied me to the neurologist, usually staying at home to care for our baby daughter. She insisted on accompanying me this time, leaving Eliza with my mum.

My visits to the neurologist tended to follow a particular pattern. He would greet me at the front desk and we'd enter his consulting suite, exchanging pleasantries about the weather, family and work. When seated, he'd ask me how things were going and whether I felt that my symptoms had changed. Then he'd test my reflexes, muscle strength, dexterity and so on.

On this occasion however there were few pleasantries and no physical examination. After we recounted our frightening experience at the restaurant, and probably after observing the way I entered his suite, he duly informed us that in his opinion we had exhausted all other possibilities and the most likely diagnosis was Motor Neurone Disease.

I had no real understanding of what this meant, and told him so.

He explained that it is a very serious condition for which there is no treatment or cure. He said that my symptoms would in all likelihood continue to progress, initially to paralysis, and, as a result, I would die. He gave me two to three years.

The news was delivered like a bombshell.

Our initial reaction was one of total shock and incomprehension. In hindsight it was probably the reason he offered little comfort or succour. Certainly the look on my face must have reflected the emotional chasm of my mind. I was completely and utterly devoid of any feelings whatsoever. I was encountering a surreal out of body experience with the whole scene being acted out before me in which I was not a player but viewing from on high. It was as if this terrible news was being delivered to a couple I did not know and it had little impact on me.

Lee was similarly stunned into silence.

We didn't ask questions about what to do next.

We didn't ask about second opinions.

We just sat, numbly, and listened.

After our consultation, I stood up, smiled, shook the doctor's hand and thanked him for his time. He could have told me that an ingrown toenail caused my ailment and my reaction would have been the same. Perhaps my only response on an emotional level was an empathic one in that I actually felt sorry for him for having to deliver such bad news.

In the following years I did become somewhat critical of the manner in which he delivered this devastating news.

While I can understand that there is no way to cushion the blow of such a distressing diagnosis, and I certainly respect the candid and informative nature in which he told us of the likely prognosis, I suppose my primary criticism is that there was no emotional or personal support offered immediately after the news was delivered.

During the drive back to my mother's house there was an unusual silence between Lee and I. We were so stunned that we simply didn't know what to do or say.

I recall making a feeble attempt at a joke, something to the effect that our meeting didn't go exactly to plan.

I remember both of us repeatedly asking each other, 'What are we going to do now? What are we going to do?' and finding no answers.

I remember too that there were a few deep sighs and many expletives used as we began to grapple with the enormity of our situation.

And it was our situation from now on. Up until this point, I had been dealing with a physical problem, my problem, but from this moment forward my problem became a family issue and I have never since regarded it as anything else. I don't regard myself as living life in isolation to others – I never have, and immediately after my diagnosis I understood that my illness would have a devastating and lasting effect on Lee, Eliza, extended family, friends and colleagues. Indeed, the minute Lee and I walked back through the door at my mum's place and saw Eliza, we were jolted out of our stunned shock and numbness and both broke down.

But I also understood that if we were going to fulfil our dreams and goals and fight for as long as we could,

I would need the support of these people. In the weeks and months ahead I was to find out just how painful this news would be to those who care about Lee, little Eliza and me. To say they rallied around is an understatement of massive proportions and does not do justice to their extraordinary response to our plight - but more about this later. To regard it as my problem would be to deny the enormous emotional and practical implications of the disease on others, particularly Lee. To this day I believe my illness has had a far greater impact on her than on me.

Bernard the go-ahead to inform the College Executive of my condition and to a person they were equally as accommodating and kind.

Throughout the remainder of 2001, I didn't inform the staff of my illness but as my speech became impaired they obviously knew something was up. I heard rumours that some staff had caught wind of my predicament but, to their credit, they made no mention of it, acceding to my wish for privacy and my desire to adopt the 'business as usual' approach. Not only had work become my principal means of escape from our situation, I also didn't want anything to impede my enjoyment of what had been to date the most rewarding phase of my career. I was so enjoying working with these kids and this staff I didn't want anything to jeopardise it – not MND, not anything.

When the younger kids made mention of my slurred speech, as kids do, I casually reassured them that I had not been to the pub for lunch but had a neurological dis-order which meant messages didn't get from my brain to my muscles properly. I was quite open and honest in my description but just didn't give the condition a name. They seemed quite unperturbed. Obviously my intellect hadn't been affected as I was lucid and on my game. If only they knew how dog-tired I was, I am sure my Year 9 Health Education class would have lurched onto the front foot and given me a pasting when my defences were down.

I had the pleasure of working with many fine students in the Year 12 Class of 2001, but none as exceptional as the College Captains, Jacqui McCudden and John-Michael McLindon. I felt a special connection with them and together we grew into our roles. They were strong leaders and were obviously held in high esteem by their peers, often treading the difficult line between the expectations of me as a teacher and an administrator and those of their colleagues. As the year wore on, and my speech began to fail, I developed a reliance on them as intermediaries by turning assemblies over to them and having them run all over the school for me. I trusted them unequivocally and they never let me down. I believe our connection was born out of their understanding and compassion for my battle, though I never expressly told them. I am proud to say that we still share a bond and I will be forever indebted to them.

Five months after my diagnosis I undertook the last of my formal duties for the year as Year 12 Coordinator, which was the final Mass for Year 12, followed by an awards ceremony. This was perhaps the single most touching and emotional experience of my time as their Coordinator. The awards were called College Colours, and these were certificates presented as reward and recognition for those who consistently demonstrated very high levels of moti-vation, strong evidence of positively enhancing social relationships, participated in key College activities, and who achieved to an outstanding level. I was blown away by the reverence with which they celebrated the Mass and the sheer joy and appreciation of their colleagues' accomplishments during the awards ceremony.

As I stood before them and some visiting parents and staff to conduct the ceremony, I was overcome by the sense of community that we, students and staff, had engendered in the group, and I was satisfied with the role I had played. I was able to walk from the position content that I had done my best under very trying circumstances and with the feeling that a few students had benefited along the way.

Along with the Mount Lilydale community, my family and friends became absolutely central to my life in the months following my diagnosis and I looked to them and sought out their support in any way I could. Actually it was Lee who really taught me the value of friends and family by her absolute devotion to them. She is the perfect daughter, sister and friend because she always seeks to strengthen these relationships through word and deed; never having a bad word to say about anyone and going out of her way to help, support and encourage. I owe everything to her for maintaining our relationships with friends and family whilst I was taking them for granted.

The day after I was diagnosed she began to reach out, not to call in favours, but to inform people of our situation because obviously they would want to know. This type of response was foreign to me. I was not used to actively seeking out such support and - truth be known - didn't really feel I was deserving of it. From day one, the phone was ringing off the hook and the doorbell running hot as people sought ways to offer their support. Lee sent to everyone a flyer from the Motor Neurone Disease Association about an up-coming information evening and while I did not attend, embarrassingly the room was overflowing with our family and friends. People were literally lining the walls and sitting on the floor. To start the evening the facilitator asked everyone in the room to individually introduce themselves and state why they were there. Apparently the catch-cry throughout the

very long introductory session was, 'My name is ………..
and I'm here for Pete.'

One of the topics discussed was how family and friends
could support someone who is suffering from MND and
their immediate family in the short, medium and long
term. No sooner had the meeting been adjourned, various
individuals and groups were off plotting their response.

A close friend, Marita Scully, had the wonderful idea
to hold a comedy night and enlisted the help of my cousin
Damian Callinan, a brilliant comedic talent on television
and in theatres, to raise money for the Victorian Motor
Neurone Disease Association. Marita poured her heart,
soul and considerable talent into organising the evening
and, on what was an awesome night, raised over $12,000
to help in the fight against MND.

CHAPTER 16

A NEW YEAR

HEADING INTO 2002 I began planning with Mount Lilydale Principal, Bernard Dobson, what my role at the school would continue to involve. From his point of view, there was no question of me not returning, despite being completely within his rights not to have offered me a position, given that I probably couldn't see a full teaching load through to the end of the year. We ended up settling on a 60% teaching load comprising a Year 12 Homeroom, Year 12 Political Studies, Year 11 Legal Studies and two Year 10 Religious Education classes with the remainder made up supervising Year 11 study and some HR policy review.

For the first time in many years I started 2002 free of the shackles of administrative duties, though fraught with uncertainty about how much of the year I would see through. Again, Bernard made the very generous concession that I was welcome to drop classes as they became too arduous.

The Religious Education classes were always going to be hard work. Year 10s are often high maintenance and Year 10 Religious Education all the more so. Such classes need not only thorough planning, but active teaching and this is where I would normally thrive. I love nothing more than to bound up and down the aisles theatrically, challenging ideas, provoking thought and engaging the students much like Danny Kennelly and Peter Molinari did to me. It is such an energising experience to connect with a group of people, eyes wide in anticipation of every word, minds open to new ideas. I imagine it to be the same experience shared by stage actors – a kind of opiate that draws you into its clutches and holds you in its vice-like grip. There's nothing quite like the feeling of self-satisfaction, after the bell has gone and the kids have been dismissed, of knowing that you just made a difference.

This had been my drug of dependence for many years but from now on I would have to be shrewder with my bag of tricks.

I didn't have the energy for such antics any longer and my speech wouldn't allow the usual diatribes.

I just became too tired and started slurring my words, or talking through my nose thanks to my weakening soft palate.

In the past, when pressed for time by the responsibilities of co-ordination, I sometimes flew by the seat of my pants and got away with poor planning and preparation. I suppose experience and a bank of curriculum resources built up over many years will afford you this luxury. In teaching circles we refer to it as the Six Step Lesson Plan

– that is, over your last six steps before you enter the classroom, you give some thought to what you are going to teach and how you are going to teach it.

Now, teaching had become more difficult and far more physically taxing than even in the early times as a graduate. I needed to adapt my approach and embrace a more student-centred methodology.

I quickly learnt through self-preservation to tailor my classes differently, handing discussion and other tasks over to the students while I became more of a facilitator, often conducting classes sitting on a vacant student desk at the back of the room. Even then, for all of my classes, I needed to arrive 10 minutes early, enter the empty classroom and go through a series of relaxation exercises in preparation for the next 50 minutes.

In the end though I couldn't stem the tide and by May 2002, I had to hand over my two Year 10 classes. As if he hadn't already done enough, Bernard Dobson, the Principal of an organisation with over 130 employees and 1500 students, stepped into the breach and took on one of those classes.

At the end of the first semester – 12 months after I was diagnosed – I had to make the heartbreaking decision to drop my Legal Studies class. These were beautiful kids and I felt as though I were abandoning them, albeit into the hands of a wonderful teacher and seasoned professional, Andrew Feher, who had to reconfigure his own teaching load to accommodate me. They had come a long way in a short period and I enjoyed the dynamics of the group, with its colourful mix of larger-than-life personalities. There was a fair smattering of brains amongst them too, which kept me on my toes and made for a challenging examination of legal issues. Andrew was also an Outdoor Education teacher, which was fortuitous as his duties pertaining to camps and the like meant he was often away, allowing me to go back in and stand before my class. I missed them terribly and our reunions were always very pleasant and reaffirming experiences for me.

I was so overwhelmed by Mount Lilydale's profuse and unreserved espousal that I was moved to write the following letter:

5 July, 2002

The Executive
Mount Lilydale Mercy College
Anderson Street
Lilydale, 3140

To the Executive,

It is very important to me that I express my most sincere appreciation to you all for your support over the past year.

For many years throughout the 1990s I had a burning desire to return to the College after having taught here from 1987 until the end of 1991. It was always my belief however, that to do so would most likely result in feelings of disappointment that the College was no longer as I had so fondly remembered it. In many ways I was right. Things have changed but I am not the slightest bit disappointed, let down or disillusioned by the College and the people in it that I have again come to know and love.

When I returned in April last year I could not have known how events were to unfold. I was healthy, enthusiastic and keen to make my mark. Instead, within a matter of months, I was dealing on a personal level with issues that consumed every ounce of my being. I tried not to let this impact on my work but eventually the physical implications of my illness began to take hold. To say that the last twelve months have been a challenge is an understatement of massive proportions. I feel so guilty that my misfortune has been brought to bear on all of you and the College.

Throughout the latter part of last year I was keen to keep news of my illness from the general staff as I did not want it to distract from my important work as Year 12 Coordinator. The students had to be the emphasis. Nor did I want anyone making allowances for me (even though thankfully many were made). At every step of the way you (the Executive) respected my wishes and were quietly supportive of my situation, seeking to make life easier for me in any way you could.

This year you have exceeded my wildest dreams. My work is so important to me and, I suppose like most of us, it essentially defines who I am. This insidious disease will eventually get the better of me but that doesn't really matter. I have a loving wife, beautiful daughter and you have allowed me the opportunity to keep doing what gives me a sense of dignity and self-worth. You will never know what this opportunity means to me or how grateful I am. Bernard, when I shed some tears in your office it was not because of any sense of self-pity – I will never allow myself that luxury. It was because I was so moved by your compassion and thoughtfulness. As you keep saying, this is a Catholic school, but I am fully aware of the practical and financial implications of your decisions at executive level and what you are doing for me goes well beyond any measure of Christian charity.

I am sorry to take up your valuable time but to express these sentiments to you personally would get very messy! Sooner or later the time will come when I can't go on. On that day know that my family and I will remain eternally grateful and indebted to you all for your amazing support and encouragement. I only hope that somehow I will find a way to make this up to you.

I go to bed every night thanking God for the wonderful gifts he has given me. Not least of which is the incredibly good fortune to have returned to Mount Lilydale Mercy College.

Yours sincerely,

Peter Anderson

CHAPTER 17

I'LL DO IT MY WAY

B Y JUNE 2002, 12 months since my diagnosis, my lability had started to cause me problems. Lability is one of the insidious conditions brought about by MND and is characterised by the inability to control your emotional responses. People with emotional lability have relatively uncontrollable episodes of laughter, crying or both. The episodes either do not have an apparent motivating stimulus or are triggered by a stimulus that would not have led the person to laugh or cry prior to the onset of MND. A mildly amusing joke may render one rolling in the aisles while a touching episode of the television drama *All Saints* may reduce you to a snivelling mess.

I went to see a doctor about altering some medication I had been prescribed in an attempt to bring my lability under control and during the course of our conversation she asked me if I was angry at having been dealt this hand. A few days prior to visiting the doctor I bumped into an old work colleague who was fighting his own battle with cancer. He asked me if I was 'through the angry stage yet'. I had been thinking a lot about this. My study of psychology taught me that there are a number of stages of grief and that the length of time within any one stage will vary depending on the individual. I must have missed the following lectures that explained why some people don't necessarily experience some or all of these stages.

I had felt many things over the previous 12 months, but anger was not a dominant emotion. Fear, yes fear was pretty high on the agenda, as was concern for the well-being of Lee and our then baby daughter, Eliza. I feared that I would only be known, and remembered, as a sick person. I feared that Eliza wouldn't get to see who I really was as a person and experience the qualities I wanted to share with her as her dad. I feared the financial implications of being unable to work and what that might mean for Lee and Eliza's security and stability. I worried about my ability to cope with the diagnosis and disease itself.

Every now and then I would allow myself the luxury of feeling frustrated at my inability to do all the things I used to do. I did question my spiritual beliefs and challenged my values but I cannot recollect ever experiencing feelings of anger. What is there to be angry at? To whom or at what would I direct my anger? God?...Medical science?...Environmental pollutants? This seemed fairly inane to me. Wouldn't it make more sense to direct my energies towards positive things? To become angry would have meant either directing my anger inwards or directing it towards those near and dear to me (collateral damage seems to be the buzz-word these days). Surely this would be counter-productive, I thought.

I remember someone saying to me that 'nobody said life was fair.' One year on, how true that was. Throughout the ages terrible things have befallen wonderful people all over the world. That's not fair either. To dwell on my situation would have made life unmercifully difficult to bear, so I chose not to be angry or bitter at the cards I had been dealt. I thanked God for my loving wife, beautiful daughter and my incredible support network.

Of course I had my down times and there would be many more to come. I loathed the effect this terrible disease was having on those around me but I vowed not to let it change who I was. I was told that MND would eventually kill me. The way I saw it, this reality narrowed down my choices somewhat. I could be consumed by the belief that my cross is too heavy to bear or I could get on with living.

To me the choice was that simple.

CHAPTER 18

COMING CLEAN

HAVING NOW DROPPED my two Year 10 classes and my Year 11 Legal Studies, I was left with a solitary Year 12 Political Studies and my beloved Year 12 Homeroom to start the second semester of 2002. It was now time for me to come clean about my illness to my politics students and ask for their assistance if I was to help them through to the end of the year.

I cannot begin to express how difficult this was.

I didn't want to burden them but felt they needed reassurance that I would see them through. Anyway, by now word had well and truly got out and it was the least I could do to show some faith and be honest with them. No doubt, they too would have been concerned about being left teacherless with only 13 weeks left in their VCE.

I rehearsed my spiel over and over in my mind and entered my Political Studies class full of trepidation. Ten minutes prior to completing the lesson I called them to attention and laid it all before them, reassuring them that I would see them through to their exams and they were not to worry. Should they feel in any way disadvantaged, however, I would step aside and let somebody else take over.

I am pleased to say I received their resounding vote of confidence and, together, we ploughed ahead into the rigours of the course. I was delighted by their approach to their studies and their compassionate response to me, as though we were all in this together.

The next step was to explain my illness to my homeroom. This was a different matter altogether as they were particularly special to me, more so than any other group in my teaching career.

This group gelled right from the outset. Made up of disparate individuals, I had the first inkling of their exceptionality in late February when we attended a four-day retreat at Mount Macedon.

There were five or six very strong characters who seemed to care nothing for peer pressure and quickly set about extracting the most from the experience that they could. They led from the front, challenged apathy amongst their colleagues, and set a tone that allowed me to fashion a cohesive, dependable and integrated team. I grew to love every one of the 21 students in Year 12 Blue and I consider myself privileged to have worked with such fine people – many of whom still visit Lee, Eliza and I today. Watching over their development into the sort of people who their parents would be proud of has been undoubtedly one of the most treasured experiences in my life.

But I needed to level with them too. I had already

softened them a month prior by asking Dianne De Munk, their co-ordinator and English teacher, to explain that I was battling with some serious health issues. I had been procrastinating because I was fearful of my inability to tell them without ending up a blithering mess. I didn't want them to feel sorry for me. In fact, I didn't want this to be about me at all.

The purpose of me telling them was first and foremost to allay any of their worries and to let them know I was fine and would support them through to the end of the year. I was also, perhaps audaciously, aware of the esteem in which they held me and needed to set straight any fears of my imminent demise. They had obviously been witness to the progression of the disease and I had begun to use a crutch. Also, we had become so close that I just wanted to share my struggle with them in the same way I had with family and friends.

I breathed an enormous sigh of relief after the deed was done and felt a weight had been removed. At least I felt that the focus had been shifted and I could now concentrate on the kids.

As the end of the year grew near, I began to think about how I could send them off into the world with a lasting image of our year together and with a proclamation of how they had helped me. In a sense I wanted to dot the I's and cross the T's on my career and make a statement about what it meant to me to spend my final year of teaching with them. I hadn't realised until my disastrous foray into business how much teaching meant to me, how good I was at it, and how it shaped me as a person. And I couldn't have wished to go out on a richer, more resounding note than in this place with these kids. I was utterly fulfilled and fully rewarded.

I decided to write each student a personal letter that I distributed on the last day. It was a masterstroke, the best thing I ever did and the poignant feedback I received from the students and their parents more than justified the huge investment of time and effort in compiling them.

Unfortunately at their graduation ceremony I was unable to walk onto the stage and present my class. I was however able to greet, shake hands and, in some instances, embrace them from the foot of the stairs as they walked up to accept their certificates. Two of the students, Natarsha Piper and Luke Evans, remained on stage and gave the most beautiful speeches in my honour before all the students, their parents and their families. They spoke of the impact I had had on their lives and of their admiration, appreciation and affection. I was thankful that Lee was there to hold my hand because otherwise my emotions would have completely consumed me. Overwhelmingly though, I experienced a profound sense of pride that these two students had developed to a point that they were standing in front of 600 people with such confidence and poise to express those beautiful words.

It's very hard for me to put into words my appreciation for what Bernard and Mount Lilydale Mercy College gave me in the 18 or so months following my diagnosis. And I know without a shadow of a doubt that if I had returned to Salesian College they would have done the same. Not because I brought anything in particular to these institutions, but because of who they are and what they stand for. Mount Lilydale gave me the opportunity to achieve absolute fulfilment in my professional life; something many people strive for all their lives, but never achieve. Holistically, though, they gave me even more.

So much of who I am is associated with my work – I define myself as a teacher. The successes I had over my last 18 months and the opportunities for affirmation made me profoundly happy and, as I attempted to express to the College Executive, gave me a sense of self-worth and dignity. I'd never have dreamt that I would be hanging up my boots at the age of 37, but equally I could not have wished for a more gratifying finale.

Michael Johnston, the Head of Senior School and a person for whom I have the utmost respect and admiration, was charged with the responsibility of expressing the farewells on behalf of the staff. These were his words on my departure in December 2002:

"I have been asked to say a few words which try to capture just what Peter Anderson means to so many people within the community of Mount Lilydale Mercy College. Whilst I have made quite a few speeches to acknowledge the work of people at this school, I feel rather inadequate when it comes to this one. I say this for two reasons.

Firstly, words cannot do justice to the person that is Peter Anderson. I have always thought of him as the most kind and decent man I have ever known. From the very first time he arrived at this school, he won over everyone who had dealings with him because of the way in which he always made time for people and nothing was ever too much trouble. To this day those same qualities are still apparent.

One staff member in particular was completely won over. So much so that she went on to marry him, much to the disappointment and annoyance of many senior female students at the time as well as a couple of female members of staff, but that is another story. In the annals of Mount Lilydale, it was a fairytale romance given that Leanne is a former student of this school.

The second reason why I feel rather inadequate in speaking this morning is due to the words spoken by two members of Peter's 12 Blue Homeroom at the recent Year 12 Graduation ceremony. Natarsha Piper and Luke Evans spoke on behalf of so many of us when they expressed their gratitude and admiration for Peter. The word 'inspiration' was used by both of them as they spoke about the way Peter had touched their lives. That night I felt very proud to be a part of this school community. The students' speeches were published in last week's Newsletter. Do yourself a favour and take the time to read it.

Peter's involvement with Mount Lilydale stretches back to 1987 and takes in two distinct periods. 1987 – 1992 and then from 2001 until the present. Whilst there was a ten-year gap it was as if nothing had changed the day he returned last year. The same qualities that made him such a brilliant and admired teacher were still in evidence.

Leah Hill (former Campus Co-ordinator of McAuley Campus) remembers Peter's first day at the school. She had lunch duty in the Quadrangle and as can often be the case, it was rather lively. This was in the days when the students had to sit down on the old wooden slat benches to eat their lunch. This fresh faced young man approached Leah and said, 'what can I do to help?' This would capture for many of us, the sort of person Peter is. In more recent times nothing has changed. A Year 12 assembly in the Lecture Theatre or Centennial Hall would see Peter make his way there, not because he had a particular thing to do, but just simply because he wanted to be there for other people. Forget about his own level of discomfort involved in being there, given that it may have taken him ten minutes to walk the distance from the staff study to the assembly venue.

Around the time Peter commenced here, Sister Beth (then Principal) provided the staff with the snooker table. The famous snooker tournament was born. The first name to appear on the trophy was Peter Anderson. That was in the days when there were real snooker players on staff - names such as Anderson, Evans, Carrick and Johnston are spoken of in reverent terms. The players of today just don't measure up!

In my office I recently discovered a photo of the very first staff cricket team to play the Mount Evelyn veterans. Peter opened the bowling for that team which was affectionately known as 'The Invincibles', captained by our own Don Bradman (Terry Dunn). The photo has a cracked frame which probably reflects the current condition of many of the members of that team. I can think of no better place for that photo to reside than on Peter's desk at home, broken frame and all.

An important part of Peter's early time at this school involved working at the Mercy Conference Centre at Mornington where we would take homeroom groups for retreat experiences. Peter was silly enough to admit to having his endorsed bus licence so he lost count of the number of times he travelled that road to and from Mornington. Sister Beth was also acutely aware of the skills Peter had in working with young people in the retreat setting and he was an integral part of a fantastic program. Fifteen years later I was fortunate enough to attend this year's Year 12 retreat with Peter and his beloved 12 Blue. I can vouch for the fact that he has lost none of his skill in this area. The complete trust and respect he had for each student in that class had to be seen to be believed, let alone the way in which they repaid him. It was a privilege for Tania Hawthorne and myself to be present for those three days.

Peter is a man of tremendous faith and great character. I have met two of his brothers and they are the same. It must have been something in the water at the Anderson household. Peter to me represents so much of what our gospel mission is. Not only has he been able to gain the respect of the students he works with, as evidenced by the connection he had with the 2001 Yr 12 students that he co-ordinated for Semester Two, he actively seeks out the lost sheep and protects the vulnerable. One young man from last year owes so much to Peter. A student so much at risk, that without Peter's nurturing he probably would not be alive today. The parable of the lost sheep was written with Peter Anderson in mind.

To know that you have made a difference in the life of at least one person must be the most rewarding aspect of a teaching career.

Peter, you have touched the lives of so many people in ways you cannot begin to know.

In more recent times we have attempted to travel a

more difficult road with you. The words of Luke Evans from Graduation best sum up our feelings:

Inspiring.
Selfless.
Courageous.

Each of us has our own story about Peter that would support these words.

Earlier this year some of us would have heard a person with MND, David Ingliss, speak about his condition on the TV show *The Panel.* As he outlined the way in which it could weaken the body but not the mind or the spirit I was overcome just thinking about Peter.

Life is very much about the triumph of the human spirit. Faced with similar circumstances, how many of us would present for work each day never asking for any allowance to be made and taking offence should any be offered? The courage that Peter has displayed may have gone unnoticed by some of us. Peter has not allowed us to see that he has struggled. Where do you gain your strength from? We cannot begin to understand.

If Peter was leaving here today to take up a teaching position at another school, the words you are hearing would be much the same. The onset of MND has not provided him with the qualities I have spoken about. It has just allowed us to witness them in different and very special ways.

Peter may be ending his classroom teaching but he will continue his links with the school. He has offered to do online tutoring for the senior students and Bernard has plans for him to be involved in policy development.

Your attitude is best summed up by a verse that you had pinned on the side of your desk in the Barak Staff Study. You can thank Dianne de Munk for pinching this.

'This can be a good day or a bad day – my choice.
I can be happy or sad – my choice.
I can complain or I can cope – my choice.
Life can be a chore or a challenge – my choice.
I can take from life or give to life – my choice.
If all things are possible,
How I deal with those possibilities is – my choice!'

Peter, thank you for all you have given to this school.

Enjoy the extra time you now have at home with Leanne and your beautiful daughter, Eliza.

You are truly an inspiration for us all."

As I strode to my car having said my goodbyes, with the fresh smell of jasmine and roses being carried on the breeze and the beautiful Yarra Valley sprawled out before me, I was content. For me, teaching is a noble profession – decent, dignified and pure.

CHAPTER 19

STRUGGLES AND SILVER LININGS

FOLLOWING MY DEPARTURE from Mount Lilydale, the disease progressed relentlessly and all measure of positive thinking, diet, medication and prayer seemed to count for naught. MND is a most hideous illness and I wished I didn't have it. Every night, although I thanked my God for the day and asked that He "give me this day my daily bread", I would also pray that He lift this colossal cross from my shoulders and those of my loved ones. Every single morning I would wake to the hope of marginally better flexibility, intelligible speech and greater independence. Every single morning I would wake in the full expectation that the day would be better than yesterday, but it never was.

My lability was worsening and my speech was increasingly restricted. And, while I had been able to walk unassisted for twelve months before I needed a crutch, the pace of muscular decline was so rapid that six months later, by

December 2002, I required a walking frame. The falls became too frequent and way too dangerous to hold out any longer. Eliza was a toddler by this stage and though I could still hold her if I was sitting down, I couldn't pick her up when standing and I certainly couldn't chase after her. Fortunately I still had good movement in my hands and relished the opportunities to be the 'hands-on' dad I always wanted to be - arts, craft, Play Doh, drawing - you name it, I made sure I did it.

Around this time I also had to give up driving. I started to ask Lee to drive to places on the weekends and gradually it extended to every occasion. I no longer felt able to control the car safely.

In late 2002, our dear friends Mark and Lynne Evans and Michael and Megan Poulton placed a proposal before Lee and I to hold a fundraiser to help us begin to make necessary alterations to our home. At the time, we needed rails on the front verandah (although the occupational therapist sent to assess our place could not understand that we wanted ornate rails to fit in with the rest of the house) and ramps leading into the front of the house.

It was very difficult at the time to accept such charity but we were won over by their enthusiasm. The proposal involved assembling a committee of family and friends to organise a ball and charity auction. As plans began to take shape, and with over 25 people on the committee, it became evident that this was going to be a grand affair. As I walked into the Box Hill Town Hall on 16 May 2003, I was physically and emotionally overwhelmed by what confronted me.

Literally hundreds of auction items adorned the foyer

and the hall was beautifully set up to cater for at least 450 people. At that moment my emotions were wavering between excitement, exhilaration, bewilderment, dread, and unqualified embarrassment. Above all, however, my overriding emotion was an overwhelming sense of humility. I cannot begin to express how difficult it was for me to be there. It is not in my nature to reach out in such a way and I was particularly mortified by all the fuss. Lee, on the other hand, was positively glowing and looked absolutely radiant, exuding happiness and confidence everywhere she went.

Earlier that same year my friends and colleagues at Salesian College organised a Trivia Night and auction to help us out financially. Again I was so overwhelmed and emotional by the outpouring of generosity and support that - at the end of the evening - I couldn't contain my emotion and wept uncontrollably in the arms of my former colleague, Steve Beckham, who had largely organised the whole thing. Similarly, Lee's school, Sacre Coeur, also held a Trivia Night attended by staff and the College community.

How many people are fortunate enough to experience such tangible expressions of love directed towards them in their lifetime?

CHAPTER 20

HOW DO YOU EAT AN ELEPHANT?

IN 2004 NEIL Kearney asked me to write something about inspiration. He'd previously written a newspaper article on our battle with MND and, after we met, he encouraged me to continue writing, often challenging me with particular issues. 'What inspires and motivates us?' he asked. I thought for a long time about the topic and couldn't help but think 'how the bloody hell should I know?' I kept reasoning, 'I know what motivates me, but I can't speak for everyone else.'

Let me say from the outset that I believe inspiration and motivation to be two distinctly different yet related things. To be inspired to some kind of behaviour or creative thought, to my way of thinking, implies the existence of some external stimulus. Perhaps a person or circumstance inspires an individual to action. Motivation, on the other hand, entails the interest or stimulus for the behaviour coming from within. That is, the reason for doing something or behaving in some way is based more on feelings or enthusiasm.

I said the two are related because the reason for doing something or behaving in some way i.e. stimulus for motivation, may well be that which inspires us. An inspirational person or a quote may motivate us to achieve something extraordinary. Sometimes, however, the motivating factors can be external. Say, for instance, an individual perceives social forces that then determine how she or he behaves. We are all subject to the pressure of social expectations and mores that determine, to a large extent, our behaviour.

I am motivated by the desire to do things correctly – whether in sport, work, family or social life. In fact, this desire is so strong in me it has sometimes actually hindered my ability to take on new challenges for fear of not being able to meet the rigors of the task and hence, failing. Fortunately I saw this flaw early and took evasive action, but it still creeps up on me every once in a while so I have to be on my toes. This awareness of my own fear of failure, especially when I was in the work environment, enabled me to check myself accordingly.

The desire to do things right was never as apparent as on the sports field. I hated making mistakes there, particularly when others depended on me getting it right. I felt the pressure to perform very keenly in this situation, particularly in my cricket as I usually opened the bowling.

My desire to do things correctly means I have to be very careful in my expectation of others, especially in my expectations of Eliza. I am mindful of the need to let her make her own mistakes and grow through them into a resilient and strong person, as hard as that sometimes may be. My dad was often critical of us as kids, probably as a result of his own perceived shortcomings, and I am determined not to do likewise to Eliza.

Often people are motivated by fear. Fear of failure, fear of conflict, fear of harm, fear of derision, and fear of ostracism from social groups. Why do we all obey the road rules? Sure, to a certain extent it's because we agree to a social contract and understand that to do otherwise would be dangerous to us, our families and other road users. On the other hand, the Transport Accident Commission in Victoria has spent millions upon millions of dollars convincing us that it's just a matter of time before we get caught. To some degree we adhere to road rules because we fear the big arm of the law will smite us if we transgress.

As a professional and a leader, fear of conflict challenged me often. I was confronted daily by situations where I had to approach staff about their performance or make decisions that I knew were going to be less than popular. Thankfully I'm not a particularly abrasive fellow and most people saw me for what I was, a young bloke just trying to do his best in a tough job. On the odd occasion when I had to stand my ground and fight it out, I kept a calm exterior that belied my uncertainty and lack of confidence. Most importantly, I grew to recognise what was driving my behaviour, which I guess is a product of experience, maturity and introspection. This recognition continues to give me some idea of how to control emotions and harness their power. It also allows me the option of nipping automatic behaviour in the bud and not being a complete slave to my environment and reacting to every stimulus. Age has its advantages in this regard. As we become more emotionally mature we are able to learn about the things that motivate and inspire us. We don't become victims to our own whims and fancies as often as when we were young. The operative word here is emotional maturity and, of course, not all adults achieve this.

Much of my time as a Coordinator and teacher was spent dealing with kids who were at the inclination of their environment. They simply went where it influenced them. Driven by peer pressure or the next 'must-have' commodity, they had no motivation for existing beyond the here and now. There were those who simply reacted, whether violently, heatedly, excitedly or despondently. They reacted completely on impulse and had no under-standing of why.

I found this to be my experience more often with the older students, as if they had somehow lost meaning. Whether the shit had been kicked out of them by life's experience or something catastrophic had happened, they usually had a reason for losing hope. Kids are in such a hurry to grow up these days and have ready access to all the stuff we adults rightly consider negative. We hear of binge drinking being endemic among kids as young as 13 and this has certainly been my experience. Regularly at roll-call on a Monday morning, my homeroom of Year 12s was hung over and very slow off the mark, with few exceptions. We have heard in recent times of the prevalence of recreational or party drugs, readily accessible to kids of school age who are more than willing to experiment with them. Cheaper than cannabis and even alcohol, they are the drug of choice for today's party scene. For the past 15 years, educationalists the world over have been sprouting the harm minimisation approach. I have to ask myself if we're beyond that.

Are kids any different today than in yesteryear? I believe so and that's not the ravings of an old, crusty and burnt out teacher. It is after years of experience, noticing the trends and working at the coalface. (God I miss it! I miss them. For all the heartache, frustration, disappointment and aggravation, the kids brought into my life such joy and laughter, such reward and fulfilment.) Anyway, how have they changed? Well, I think they have lost the ability to motivate themselves. Whether they are used to passive entertainment, I don't know, but they seem to expect everyone to jump through hoops for them. And if you don't, then you confirm their belief that adults can't be trusted. Of course I'm not suggesting this is the case with all kids but it is my experience with four out of every 10. I should also point out that this doesn't make them bad kids either. On the contrary, the overwhelming majority were fantastic kids who just lacked a particular skill: they have lost sight of their goals, or didn't have any to start with.

As a Coordinator at the Year 12 level I used to spend a great deal of time on goal setting. At level assemblies I used to bang on about this topic until I was blue in the face.

'How do you eat an elephant?' I'd ask.

'In very small pieces,' was the response I'd eventually give.

I fervently believe that if kids have realistic goals they can achieve them, given guidance and a safety net. There's nothing erroneous in setting the bar high, in fact it's criminal not to encourage students to strive beyond their preconceived capabilities. If you don't have goals, how on earth will you know how to get there? It seems pretty straightforward to me and that is at the root of the cause of young people drifting through their adolescence aimlessly, underachieving and failing to meet their potential. Worse, they become susceptible to pressure from peers and the insidious forces of depression. We all need a compass, something to guide us through life's journey with its ups and downs, its pitfalls and its triumphs. If you like, we can call this compass 'values', and young people are in need of help in defining them more than ever.

My favourite piece of writing on the theme of goal setting comes from John Naber, the 100m Backstroke Olympic gold medallist in 1976. I gave this piece to my homeroom every year and also to any Legal Studies or Political Studies classes I was taking. I would revisit it many times throughout the course of the year to check if they were on the right track.

GOAL SETTING FOR
CONTINUOUS IMPROVEMENT

In 1972 Mark Spitz won seven gold medals, breaking seven world records! I was at home watching him on my living room floor. I said to myself at the time 'Wouldn't it be nice to be able to win a gold medal...to be able to be a world champion in Olympic competition...' So right then I had this dream of becoming an Olympic Champion. **But right about then it became a goal.**

That **dream-to-goal transition** is the biggest thing I ever learned prior to Olympic competition – **how important it is to have a goal.** Certainly motivation is important. A lot of kids have motivation. 'Gee, I'd love to be great...'

My personal best in the 100 backstroke was 59.5 seconds. Roland Matthes, winning the same event for the second consecutive Olympics in 1972 went 56.3 seconds. I extrapolated his three Olympic performances and I figured that in 1976 you would have to swim 55.5 seconds to win. **That's what I figured I would have to do!** So I'm four seconds off the shortest backstroke event in the Olympic program.

It's a substantial chunk. **But because it's a goal now I can decisively figure out how I can attack that.** I have four years to do it in. I'm watching TV in 1972...I've got four years to train, so it's only one second per year. That's still a substantial chunk. Swimmers train ten or eleven months of the year so it's about one tenth of a second per month, giving time off for missed workouts.

And you figure we train six days a week, so it's only about 1/300th of a second per day. We train from six to eight in the morning and four to six at night so it's really only about 1/1200th of a second every hour!

Do you know how short 1/1200th of a second is? Look at my hand and blink when I click my fingers…OK… From the time that your eyelids started to close to the time they touched, 5/1200th's of a second has elapsed!

For me to stand back on the pool deck and say 'during the next 60 minutes I'm going to improve that much'… That's a believable dream. **I can believe in myself.** I can't believe that I am going to drop four seconds by the next Olympics…But I can believe that I can get that much faster…

…Couldn't you…Sure!

…So all of a sudden I'm moving!

John Naber
Olympic 100m Backstroke
<u>Gold Medallist 1976</u>

As much as I love the way goal setting can motivate and inspire us, it is the profusion of goodness in the world that I rejoice in more. This is by far my greatest inspiration and motivation – happiness and love. It's my motivation for everything. Sport, hobbies, work, family and social life, even my deepest thoughts; they are all driven by a desire to be happy and feel as though I am involved in something bigger and more important than just myself. Wouldn't life be terribly barren if we only looked inwards, gazing at our own navel all day long? This is what inspires me to get out of bed each day: the inspiration of others, the ordinary things that people do and say because they love me and I love them. I have never really been inspired by great feats of a sporting kind, super human endeavours or leaders shouting at me to rally to the cause.

What I find inspirational is ordinary people doing extraordinary things.

I once read Lance Armstrong's book, *It's Not About the Bike*. Though I admire everything about him, I found I couldn't at all relate to his experience. Everything about the man seemed foreign to me - his attitude to winning, his single mindedness, his brashness. He seemed superhuman and I really couldn't relate to this at all. I felt impotent reading about his triumph over testicular cancer. A man of such awesome physical and mental capacity can pull off such thing - but not I.

It's the same with Kieren Perkins' herculean effort in winning his second gold medal at the 1996 Atlanta Olympic Games. Who does that, especially when he had qualified slowest of all, and swam from lane eight?

Athletes like these are born to greatness, notwithstanding the long, arduous, and intensive work they must put in to achieve their moment of glory. I can learn important lessons from these athletes about persistence and hard work, but I cannot hope to reach their incredible heights, nor am I inspired by them.

On the other hand, there are the young ANZACs who, during the battle of the Nek in Turkey in the summer of 1915, went 'over the top' and rushed headlong into a hail of machine gun fire. Not once, but again and again, because they were ordered to and because that's what their mates were doing. According to legend, the typical ANZAC rejected unnecessary restrictions, possessed a cutting sense of humour, was contemptuous of danger, and proved himself the equal of (if not superior to) anyone on the battlefield. Many see the ANZAC spirit as having been born on that Gallipoli Peninsula in that failed eight-month campaign. Those ordinary young men did extraordinary things, and I derive inspiration from them.

In June 2004, my brothers Mark and Matt, as well as Mark's 15-year-old daughter Jessica, went on a nine-day trek to Papua New Guinea along the infamous Kokoda Track. I kept a website which I updated regularly with all the Anderson news. This is how I described their exploits on my website:

'Difficult at the best of times, the track threw up many challenges and the weather certainly didn't help matters. It rained for 5 days straight rendering the at times almost vertical track a boggy mess and swelling the rivers that had to be crossed into dangerous torrents of raging white water. For 8 nights and 9 days they battled the elements, the tropical heat, the leeches and their own doubts, to raise awareness of MND. I was particularly moved whilst viewing their video footage.

On Global MND Awareness Day they pushed themselves to get to Isurava, the site of a significant World War II battle and now one of the most sacred sites along the trail. A memorial at the site has four pillars engraved with the words Mateship, Courage, Sacrifice and Endurance.

As Matt so eloquently put it: 'all those words have such strong resonance with the fight against MND.'

I was moved to tears as they wished me well on the video camera at this site.

The Kokoda Track and the deeds that took place there form one of the most significant parts of our nation's history. As one of the trekking party said in the video: 'I have been to Gallipoli and this is every bit as moving.'

The words courage, sacrifice and endurance can equally apply to Mark on this journey. On day 3 as he was negotiating the steep track, he slipped and hurt his leg. Never one to complain, he carried on in immense pain, fearful that his injuries may require medical evacuation and, therefore, a premature end to the trek. He surmised that as long as he was not the last into camp on any day, the trek leader could not send him packing.

The day after Mark returned to Melbourne after completing the trek, he had x-rays to find a clean break in his lower leg.

Can you imagine what it must have taken to walk in mountainous terrain and through rocky, surging rivers with a broken leg for a further 5 or 6 days? Any old digger would be proud! I certainly am.

Viewing the video footage is an inspiration and I invite you all to click on the Gallery page to catch a glimpse of their adventure. Apparently Jessica is the youngest female to ever attempt the trek and did so with comparable ease. She is a very tough and determined young lady. Matt's military background obviously helped, but he too had problems with blistering, bloody, festering feet in the later stages when it rained non-stop and they were trudging through swamps, mud, slush and rivers.'

Yep, ordinary people doing extraordinary things - that's what inspires me.

CHAPTER 21

MND

As TIME WORE on the relentless nature of the physical manifestations of the illness became incredibly wearing. By 2004, just three years beyond diagnosis, my body had become grotesque and almost unrecognisable to me in terms of its limitations.

Every muscle in my body was taut and unyielding like a rusted spring. At this point even a simple sneeze would see my whole body contort violently and whatever I was holding at the time, whether a hot coffee, bowl of cereal or mobile phone, would get flung across the room, as did I.

My sleep suffered terribly and I required large doses of a muscle relaxant called Baclofen and a sedative to bring on slumber. Even then the most uninterrupted sleep I would experience was about four hours before the muscles in my legs would spasm and cramp and I would require the whole bed to roll over and relieve my aching limbs.

In this period we made the decision that Lee would no longer sleep in our bed. I detested that circumstances necessitated Lee being banished to the spare room, but for her sake and mine it was better that way. We hung on for as long as we could but in the end decided that we would both be able to better confront the day ahead with at least a few hours sleep under our belts.

I began to learn to ride through the horrible hamstring cramps which would leave me in excruciating pain, as Lee was no longer in our bed to jump into action when I grimaced and cried out in sheer agony. We still watched a bit of TV together in bed before Lee would slip off to her more comfortable digs, but every evening as she lovingly tucked me in and checked that I was OK, a little piece of me died as I lamented the loss of intimacy between people who love each other deeply.

I was still doggedly clinging to my walking frame around the house but had to relent and use a wheel chair elsewhere. I used the walking frame for as long as was humanly possible, as it provided exercise for my legs and arms. Use it or lose it, I would always say. I know people saw me as being stubborn and couldn't understand why I wouldn't utilise the aides that were available to make daily tasks a bit easier. I found it psychologically difficult to surrender more independence and felt that in doing so I was giving in and was one step closer to the grave.

Heading into 2005, my remaining physical capacity was pretty much lost or severely curtailed. I was only able to awkwardly shuffle my feet, my arms were so stiff I could not properly embrace my daughter (let alone pick her up) and my hands and fingers would clumsily render tasks that required fine motor coordination virtually impossible.

I knew with absolute certainty that in the weeks, months and years ahead it would only get worse until my muscles could no longer support my lungs, and would slowly suffocate me.

My tongue, lips and jaw were so inflexible that I could not manipulate food around my mouth, purse my lips to give a simple kiss or even speak coherently.

I can't begin to express how difficult it is to lose one's ability to communicate. From basic levels like 'can I please have a drink?' to the more profound levels, communication is what defines our humanity. It is the means by which we seek to have our primary needs met, as well as higher order needs, such as self-actualisation. American psychologist Abraham Maslow described the need for self-actualisation as "the desire to become more and more what one is, to become everything that one is capable of becoming". Individuals at this stage seek information on how to connect to something beyond themselves. That is, other people.

My inability to connect to others was incredibly frustrating and ostracising, and consigned me to the role of 'spectator' in social settings and family life, a situation I found distressing. People would try their best to include me in conversation, and initially I would respond via my 'talking machine', which lacked spontaneity and conversation, and tended to break down. I then began using a 'LightWriter', a computerised communication device that I typed into and it spoke for me. However, to awkwardly type "I love you" into my communication device, and for it to be spat back out in an electronic monotone, seemed disingenuous and I rarely took the time to do it.

Equally, being forced to conduct a relationship with Eliza, then four, through a computer was torture for both of us. I love Eliza with all my being, but during this stage I often wondered if she knew it. In the early years of her life she rarely came to me seeking solace if upset or hurt. It was no wonder though, as I had little to offer but sympathetic eyes and a comforting groan. To this day I hang out for her bedtime, when she climbs on me to give a goodnight kiss and cuddle and whisper 'I love you'. In that instant everything seems to vanish and I feel completely whole again.

There were also many other unfortunate side effects of the weakening of the muscles in my throat and mouth. My swallowing reflex became lax, causing me to pool saliva in my mouth which would then come out streaming every time I lowered my head. This was just charming when sitting at a restaurant or at someone's house for dinner. While at this stage there were not too many problems swallowing food, thin and tasteless liquids like water could go down the wrong way and cause me to gag, cough and splutter badly. My doctors feared that I would choke on food if my swallowing reflex became any slacker or if I aspirated foodstuffs into my lungs, causing infection and pneumonia.

In 2005, four years after diagnosis, my respiratory specialist raised the unpleasant and confronting topic of a Percutaneous Endoscopic Gastrostomy Tube (PEG).

Such a tube is inserted into the stomach with the aid of an endoscope and is brought outside the body through a small incision in the abdominal wall (approximately between the lower ribs) and secured with a crossbar called a bolster. Your daily caloric, fluid and electrolyte needs are provided by the administration of formula or pureed food through the PEG tube.

I needed to consider this while my lung function was still sufficient to support me through a general anaesthetic; just another one of many life-altering decisions that Lee and I were called on to make.

My lability had become crippling as my MND progressed. This was one of the most sinister of all the side effects of this disease and I would have to excuse myself from, or avoid altogether, any situation that could potentially bring on an emotional response.

While I rarely cried, I found that in any moderately amusing situation I would laugh uncontrollably and hysterically to the point where I was unable to breathe. In such situations I had been known to vomit at the table during dinner parties. I am sure you can imagine the dampener this casts over proceedings. During these fits of laughter I was far from euphoric; quite the contrary, I was exceedingly embarrassed and silently screaming for someone to help me stop this ridiculous and inappropriate laughter.

I was also petrified that my heart and lungs were going to explode.

My laugh had changed too - from a once manly, deep resonance to an embarrassing, sleazy gurgle and a snorting sound.

Overall, I avoided emotionally engaging my mind

when a conversation would head in a light-hearted direction or when a moving issue was discussed. This is one of the cruellest aspects of the disease, because it ostensibly meant that for self-preservation, I had to change who I was. No longer could I relax in the company of others, enjoy a movie, tell a joke, or just be me and enjoy the moment without having to constantly check and re-check my emotional state and get a grip on myself. All of these symptoms remain today.

The psychological and emotional implications of these symptoms were excruciating. I was regularly pissing my pants because I couldn't get to a toilet in time. I had an increased dependence on others for the most rudimentary of tasks. And then there was the changing nature of the relationship between Lee, Eliza and I - all the while knowing no treatment or cure existed.

I couldn't be the hands-on dad I knew I was capable of being. I couldn't participate at all in Eliza's playgroup or school events. I knew I wouldn't be able to coach Eliza at netball, man the barbeque at the school fete or be the timekeeper at her school sports. We could no longer go camping as a family. Those were just some of the tangible ways in which our relationships were changing. Then there were the other, deeper implications. I could no longer reach out to friends and family when they needed me – Lee had to communicate on my behalf. Sending an email was just not in my nature, when human interaction says so much more. And in turn, Lee needing to be there for me meant that we as a couple couldn't be there for others in the way we used to.

That year, my doctors had also informed me that I had

the slower form of MND, called Primary Lateral Sclerosis. While the progression of MND has to be observed in order to make this slightly more positive diagnosis, even this 'good' news seemed to be another blow; if only they had told me this was a possibility when I was giving up work so many years ago. I would have had more children to keep Eliza company. I was not sure whether this is a curse or a blessing. I felt like such a drain on those close to me, which I found intolerable.

It became exhausting having death on my mind all the time. I did allow this disease to enter my psyche and I would find myself increasingly viewing the days ahead with greater scepticism.

I would often find myself planning for my funeral and organising music, or becoming preoccupied with creating picture slideshows for after I'd gone. I guess there's nothing particularly wrong with this, as it would be irresponsible to leave Lee and Eliza in the lurch. But eventually I had to ask myself: at what point would my cynicism and negativity become counterproductive and have an adverse impact on my ability to fight?

What was of most concern to me was the potential for my increased pessimism and malaise to affect the relationships with the people I hold so dear. I have always considered myself a pretty resilient kind of bloke. Nothing much fazes me and I don't get my nose out of joint very often at all. But by 2006 a new air of pessimism had me worried. Pessimism breeds hopelessness and once all hope is lost, what else remains?

I felt myself rudderless and drifting, looking to the day without much fervour or anticipation. Where I would once bang on about 'accepting the diagnosis, not the prognosis', I was not living it. I became terribly disappointed in myself for becoming this way because I had been so strong up until this point.

It wasn't any particular event that set me on this course, as there were many during this period. One that springs to mind occurred when my parents-in-law Kevin and Maureen Wells were baby sitting me whilst Lee was at work. In such circumstances, I wouldn't tend to drink much for fear of getting caught short at the loo. On this occasion I didn't have any choice, as it was brutally hot and Lee was out for the day.

I had managed to take myself off to use my urine bottle and successfully did the deed but when placing it back on the table, being all thumbs, I tipped the contents into my bloody lap, totally drenching myself in my own piss.

I didn't know what to do.

I couldn't sit there in stinking clothes all day but equally I didn't want to call on Kevin and Maureen to get me out of my rancid clothes.

I sat there for all of ten minutes in total disbelief at what I had done, trying to find a solution, any solution, that didn't involve complete humiliation. Alas, when you are wheelchair bound and have limited use of your arms, the options are few. I had to suck it in, take one for the team, and call Kevin and Maureen.

They were fantastic and immediately swung into action. It was difficult to get me standing but we used the grab rails in the bathroom to hold my weight. So, there I was in all my glory, standing buck naked with my parents-in-law! It was a sorry sight and once they cleaned me up and dressed me, I tried to thank them but completely lost all composure.

I cried in Maureen's arms for ten minutes at what I had become.

CHAPTER 22

MY BETTER HALF - PART II

LEE AND I have never been ones to fight. In our five years of courting (that sounds such an old-fashioned word) and 16 years of marriage, I cannot think of a single incident or issue upon which we have stood toe to toe and had a significant stoush. Of course there have been times when one or the other has received the silent treatment, but we rarely let the sun go down on an argument.

Lee has always been better at the silent treatment than I - whether dispensing or receiving it, she has never let on that it bothered her. When I am on the receiving end I am often mortally wounded and, though sometimes feeling that I have no reason to be sorry, approach with my tail between my legs and attempt to talk it out. I have noticed some couples thrive on conflict, passionately voicing their dissatisfaction or difference of opinion at every juncture, often airing their dirty laundry in public, much to others' embarrassment.

Lee and I prosper on mutual understanding and respect for each other and, though Lee has a far stronger personality than I, we compliment each other beautifully. Lee is rational and I am intuitive. Lee *thinks* her way through conflict and I *feel* my way. Lee never raises her voice to me and is the epitome of control, simply shaking her head in disapproval (or worse, disappointment), whereas I am prone to grunt and snort under my breath and leave the room. Over the past ten years we have become far more adept at short-circuiting a disagreement by laughing it off as inconsequential or unimportant in the greater scheme of things.

I guess that in any successful relationship there is give and take and that's what Lee and I have always been good at (at least until the past few years). We just assumed that the first home from work would begin preparing dinner. If Eliza needed her bottle - you gave it to her. If the laundry basket was full - you did a load of washing. If you were asked out by mates – the partner would stay put and attend to the home duties. Granted, I sometimes needed to have my eyes opened to the fact that the basket was full or the dishwasher needed emptying as opposed to the far more pressing need to clean my golf clubs or rinse my wetsuit. We didn't keep a running ledger of all deposits and withdrawals in our relationship, where being in the red meant a good deed had to be repaid to the other. What goes around comes around and there was never any expectation of payback.

By the end 2005, if such a ledger existed, it would have registered an overabundance of debits on my side; in fact, I would be bankrupt. For me, this was currently the single biggest issue in our relationship at that time and it made me sick to my stomach. The entire nature of our partnership had changed. It was no longer a joint venture into which we both ploughed our resources, time and energy. Lee had become my carer, and this changed the complexion of our relationship. I was dependent on her, not only in the way I used to be for love, companionship and affection, but now also for my most basic of survival needs. Lee dressed me, washed and dried me, helped me to the toilet, got me into and out of bed (not in the way I had become accustomed!), cooked all my meals and sometimes had to feed me, and washed all my clothes. She couldn't leave me for more than a couple of hours at a stretch and was continually on tender hooks in case I fell (which happened more times than I can recall). Often when she was attending to my needs she let out a subterranean and gut-wrenching sigh, not because she begrudged helping me, but because the burden of my illness weighed so heavily upon her.

Occasionally, late at night after Eliza had gone to sleep, I heard Lee sobbing under the shower, heart-broken and despondent, feeling so alone and hopeless. This was too much to bear and tore me apart. I formed the belief that much of her suffering would moderate if I were no longer here, that she would be better off without me. I don't wish to be melodramatic here; this is just the way I have at times felt. I knew that on a rational level I was not to blame for the way things had turned out, but the fact remains that my illness has had a catastrophic effect on those closest to me; Lee most of all.

At times, my guilt would overwhelm me and I'd find

it incredibly hard to cope with these feelings.

I still don't know how to process that.

On one hand I feel so culpable but, on the other, I want to seize every minute of every day with her because I adore her, love being with her and, ultimately, she makes me happy. It's anomalous, but in many ways I love my life. I love waking to the new day with Lee and Eliza, fraught with uncertainty but buzzing with anticipation. Is this selfish? In what manner do I contribute to Lee's happiness? How can I reconcile the fact that I cause such distress to someone I love so dearly? How do I appease my feelings of complete inadequacy and of contributing nothing but a life of servitude? These are the issues I ponder in the deep of the night but the answers are never forthcoming. Perhaps I shouldn't think at all. Shit happens – don't they say?

Lee makes me happy for many reasons, not least of which is her propensity for laughter. This is what drew me to her from the start. Her broad smile, bright eyes and her willingness to 'have a go' immediately attracted me and still do. Even in the earlier years as my speech deteriorated, and despite the fact I can no longer speak now, we would still find plenty to laugh about, often directing our humour towards our situation, which I'm sure must be unsettling to some acquaintances who are not sure where to tread. Lee would sometimes make fun of my attempts at speech, which would start me giggling and ultimately render me a writhing mess.

Once, as Lee was preparing me for bed, we pondered the question of where we'd be if our roles were reversed.

"I look after you so well Pete, you could never do the

same for me," Lee said jokingly.

I conceded she was right.

"Yep, I'd have you in a nursing home and Eliza at boarding school," I joked back.

"Well, at least I could look forward to visits from you on the weekends," Lee responded dryly.

"Ah no, Saturdays would be reserved for the footy," I said, "and I'd really probably need to visit my girlfriend on Sundays."

We laughed loud and hard but in our humour we touched on the reality that I could not do for Lee what she has to do for me every day. I don't know where she finds the patience, the stamina and the will to keep giving and giving.

Neil Kearney asked what we have learned about each other on our journey. From my point of view I have learned nothing about Lee that I didn't already know. Her strength of character and her ability to care was always evident. I saw it in the way she conducted herself in both her personal and professional relationships. She gives everyone her full ear and listens empathically, embodying the belief that people should speak half as much as they listen. She does not seek to impose her will on others but they tend to fall in behind her, inspired by her quiet self-confidence, vision and willingness to do the hard yards.

They say it's not easy living with a perfectionist but I thoroughly enjoy it (most of the time). To Lee, near enough is never good enough, (sometimes at great personal cost) and, though I rarely meet these lofty standards myself, I respect immensely her desire to do so. In this regard we are a great team in that I sometimes have to apply the handbrake that she lacks, opening her eyes to the concept that she can't please all of the people all of the time. It took me years to convince her that she really didn't need to draft her students' reports twice before completing the good copy and that, really, all the food in the pantry didn't have to be perfectly lined up according to height. Lee has single-handedly kept the Asia-Pacific arm of Ikea afloat by purchasing every storage solution in their catalogue. It must be in her genes because her mum has to polish the light fittings before having visitors over.

Though I make fun of her, I respect her self-discipline and work ethic enormously. Not only does she apply these high standards to the routine in her life but also to her relationships – and, by association, this is where I come out smelling like roses.

She invests time and energy in her relationships by making an effort, even when she is flat-out, drop-down exhausted. She is loyal, dedicated to family and holds fast to the strength of her convictions. From this she will not waver. I reckon that in our current circumstances one could forgive Lee for not being as attentive to such things as birthdays, friendly gatherings or family celebrations but Lee insists on having a crack at everything – and on bringing a plate! Moreover, it is her emotional investment in these relationships that is so staunch. People love her because they know how much she loves them. They see it in deed and word – Lee puts her money where her mouth is.

I saw this from the start and in the twenty-one years

I have known her, absolutely nothing has changed. Her purity of heart is plain for all to see. If I have learned anything, it is about myself and how fortunate I am to have grown in her love, to be cradled in her loving arms. She makes me complete because she is many of the things I am not. When I look into her eyes I see reflected back at me her love and understanding.

She is my everything.

CHAPTER 23

THE PRAYER

BY 2006, I had become the definition of a 'wall flower'.

Seen but not heard at most social gatherings. Listening in on other people's conversations but not having any input - although screaming out to be heard.

Don't get me wrong, I still very much enjoyed the company of others and sought out any opportunities for social interaction, but I found my inability to contribute extraordinarily frustrating. These feelings remain the same today. When it came, however, to maintaining, strengthening and developing my close personal relationships, my inability to communicate effectively was not just frustrating but truly agonising.

Though leading busy lives, Lee and I used to be wonderful communicators. We shared hearty conversation over the dinner table or over the kitchen sink, in the car, or in bed. By now this was lost and I saw the anguish written all over Lee's face. It was clear she felt it just as acutely as I. To this day, it torments me right to my very core.

These were incredibly difficult times for me psychologically. One night I tried to say a prayer but the words just weren't forthcoming. I woke up the following morning and immediately began to write:

The Prayer

"Usually as I climb into bed I take a moment to offer thanks for the events of the day and ask for strength to meet the challenges of tomorrow. Last night, however, I couldn't find anything to be thankful for. I have lost all sense of hope and am increasingly feeling inadequate and trapped within my body.

People often speak of God's grand plan and how our prayers are answered in ways that aren't always manifestly clear to us at the time. I suppose faith is all about submitting to this grand plan but I am afraid I don't have what it takes. I despise myself for being the way I am and am intensely fearful of the road ahead. I suppose I can handle many of the physical aspects of the disease, but am currently struggling with my inability to communicate my feelings to others. It's one thing to have a terminal illness but something else altogether to have to process this reality, and the thoughts and feelings that accompany it, without the capacity to verbally communicate these to the people who are closest to me. I want to apologise to Lee and comfort her in her darker moments. I want to reassure Eliza that Dad loves her and wants to cradle her in his arms. I want to spontaneously express my sincere appreciation to my friends and family for their incredible support, without having to type a formal letter. I just want to contribute to the life of my family, my friends and my community.

I couldn't offer thanks last night because I wasn't feeling particularly grateful for the way my life has turned out, and for this I feel guilty. I know there are many millions of people who are worse off than me. But right here, right now, I see what effect this illness is having on my family and I can't bear the pain. It suffocates me like a crushing weight and I look in Lee's eyes and see that it does the same to her. She never says so, but she doesn't have to – the burden is too much and the tension too near the surface. Eliza is too young to understand and loves me unconditionally, but often, when she is upset or unhappy, she needs someone to hold her and that someone is rarely me. Now she doesn't look to me for comfort but seeks it elsewhere and this breaks my heart in a way I simply can't describe.

So how do I deal with this? The people closest and dearest to me; the people who love and support me are being crushed under the weight of this despicable illness. My strength waning, my energy sapped, my will eroded, from where can I derive my motivation? I guess the answer is in the very people I describe above – my family, my friends, my community and maybe even my God. My answer is in my prayer because every night (except last night) I invariably find so much to be thankful for – Lee's smile, Eliza's antics, an email from a friend, the girl at the local café who signals for me to take a seat and brings my café latte without me having to ask. These small things that provide life's texture, the things that constitute the 'bright side of life'. They are still as present as they have always been and now stand out in all their beauty; I just have to keep looking. It's easy to get lost in the fog of self-pity and sink into the mire of depression. I owe it to my loved ones to rise above this and return their devotion and selflessness. And I owe it to myself because I am better than this. I can't help the physical implications of Motor Neurone Disease but I determine how I let it affect me emotionally and psychologically. Any more than one option constitutes a choice and I choose to live, to contribute, and to make a difference."

Not long after writing this piece I saw a television program that raised the concept of "attraction". Why do some people seemingly have all the luck? Why do some people always seem to fall on their feet, and how come a multitude of riches befall those who are already well off? Put quite simply, the Law of Attraction says that you attract into your life whatever you think about. Your dominant thoughts will find a way to manifest. Attraction suggests that these people have a positive mindset and view the world, and their place within it, optimistically. Moreover, these people actually expect to be successful, or happy, or wealthy, or sometimes even healthy. They are so because they possess an energy that attracts these things to them. Conversely the pessimist attracts the opposite. Caustic phenomena befall their kind because their mindset is one of negativity.

Now, I'm not a particular devotee of this theory and,

like you, maybe I could pick holes in it and provide enough exceptions to the rule to debunk it. However, I believe there's no doubt that the power of positive thinking has brought me this far and watching programs such as this would often be enough to provide me with a wake-up call. As the most rudimentary tasks became more difficult, I had to surrender most of my independence and found myself slipping further into the clutches of this insidious disease. I guess I just dropped the ball for a while. I shouldn't have been too hard on myself. After all, many people would have raised the white flag long before this point.

CHAPTER 24

THE HAWKS AND MY BEST MAN

FIVE YEARS AFTER diagnosis, I was completely restricted to my chair and spending lengthy periods at home. My love for sport had largely developed into that of a spectator and the sport I have always enjoyed most to watch is Australian Rules football. In my view, there's nothing as skilful as the game of Aussie Rules played at the top level. Mind you, I enjoy the game at suburban level also. I didn't play footy beyond school as I was far too slight and did not have enough of the mongrel in me. I possessed good skills but was injured too often at the school level to contemplate senior football. I would rather face a hard and fast cricket ball than stand toe to toe with some of the Neanderthals masquerading as footballers in the local competition.

In my younger days I would follow my local club, the Forest Hill Zebras, as a number of mates were playing there. There's nothing as parochial or passionate as the local football crowd and I was always bemused at the behaviour of some people.

There was the obese woman who loved to hang over the boundary fence and scream obscenities at the umpires.

The pot-bellied and crimson-faced man who single-handedly kept the club's coffers viable through his consumption of beer. He wore the same t-shirt every week, rain, hail or shine.

The kids kicking their footballs that were oblivious to the state of the game and were chastised angrily by grumpy, pissed men when the ball was kicked into them.

There was the bloke who only had one leg. He was the loudest and the most obscene of them all.

There was Don Howell, my old neighbour who ran a wet towel out to an injured player no matter the injury! Dawn (Don's wife) who ran the canteen with the precision of a McDonald's franchise, the committee men and women who gave huge amounts of their time because they were community minded and loved to be involved.

These types of people were the lifeblood of every club – the people who bleed green and white, the colours of the club.

Then there's the people like me – the sort of person who just loves the sounds and the smells of suburban footy, needs to feel a connection to their community, share a beer and forget their troubles for a few hours on a Saturday afternoon.

Having all my life supported the Hawthorn Football Club, the day my mate and best man Mark (Evo) Evans was appointed their Football Operations Manager in 2006 was, with the exception of Eliza's birth and my marriage to Lee, probably the best day of my life.

Mark taught with me at Mount Lilydale and played many seasons in the old Victorian Football Association (VFA) as a gun mid-fielder for Prahran and Box Hill. We have shared many wonderful times together with Evo, Lynne and their kids and they remain close friends today. Evo has the most brilliant mind of anyone I have met. Plucked from near obscurity from the Melbourne Football Club where he was the Communications Manager and Player Development Manager, Hawthorn recognised a good thing when they saw it and snapped him up. (It's of no surprise to me that in 2008 the Hawks enjoyed the Premiership success that Mark envisaged when he took over the helm of the Football Department.)

The first time Evo invited Lee and I into the players' rooms was terribly exciting. Lee pushed my wheelchair down into the bowels of the Melbourne Cricket Ground. That would have been enough for me and if we had turned around and gone no further, I would have been quite satisfied. We entered the rooms and nervous antici-pation and the smell of liniment filled the air.

The players were going through their pre-match rou-tines. You could have cut the atmosphere with a knife.

Mark Williams was kicking a ball at a clock covered by wire mesh high up on a wall. He didn't miss.

Sam Mitchell, Shane Crawford and Luke Hodge were deep in conversation over to one side.

Campbell Brown was prowling back and forth like a caged lion.

Trent Croad was squatting against the wall, his massive thighs glistening with sweat and liniment.

The players started their close-in drills and the excitement level rose to a crescendo. I could feel the hair standing up on the back of my neck and it was all I could do to keep myself from crying. I was so caught up in the moment.

Unfortunately we lost that game but went down again to the rooms afterwards, this time all the more exciting as we took Eliza. I had signed Eliza up as a member of the Hawthorn Football Club when she was three years old but this was her first season going to games.

Just like my father before me, Eliza has become a dyed-in-the-wool supporter. She has all the paraphernalia. A jumper with Shane Crawford's number nine on the back, a flag which she waves vigorously at games (much to the chagrin of those sitting nearby), an assortment of membership scarves courtesy of the years she's been a member and various other bits and pieces we invariably have to gather up to go to a game. It would warm my heart to see her sitting with her nana at Hawks' games, conscientiously filling in her footy record when a goal or behind was scored. That day was getting the chance to see her idols first hand.

We were ushered out from behind the netting used to keep the masses at bay and asked to come into the inner sanctum of the locker room. The assistant coaches' kids were all knocking around and Eliza joined the fray along with Samantha Evans, who is Evo's youngest and a close friend to Eliza. We had unfettered access to the playing group and Eliza milked it for all it was worth. Before we left she had the signature of every player on her back and was beaming about the experience. She has had many similar ones since.

I can't help but think that maybe one day she will talk in the same reverent and hushed tones about the likes of Mitchell, Hodge, Sewell and Franklin as my mum did of Rose, Richards, Mann and Weideman.

It's the Anderson way.

CHAPTER 25

NEW MANTRA: OPTIMISM AND HOPE

By 2007, MND sat like a crushing weight every minute of every day. It was not at the forefront of my mind and I didn't wear it obviously on my sleeve, but it was always in the background, permeating our lives. That said, I was so proud of the way our family continued dealing with our lot in life. I was self-satisfied by my own response. In fact, I felt I had become a far healthier, more principled person than I was before.

I realised that incredible gifts had been bestowed upon me in my life and I felt blessed. I know it sounds clichéd but having the spectre of my own expiration hover over me, as well as the slow degeneration of my body, stimulated a lively awareness of the goodness in the world around me and of how fortunate I have been to share in this life. There are so many things that have become clearer, about myself, my place in the world, my impact on others and the beauty of creation. I felt I could pass beyond this world a profoundly happy and fulfilled soul.

I guess you could say that I'd become more in touch with my spiritual side. Not in a 'god' sense but in terms of another, more precious dimension to myself. Before this illness took hold, I was considerably more concerned with how others saw me. Good impressions, material belongings and job titles weighed me down. I was quick to judge others and remiss in considering my own failings. Occasionally I was a poor brother, son and mate because I conducted those relationships on my terms, in my time and under my conditions.

But by 2007, perhaps even earlier, I was manifestly more outward looking, with the luxury of not getting caught up in life's bullshit.

I would have loved to have another crack at existence unencumbered, all the baggage from this disease cast off, but I knew life didn't work out that way. I still absolutely despised the disease – I still do - and prayed the curse would be lifted from me, but I at least felt better equipped to deal with it and celebrate life beyond it. I swore I would never let it define me as a person, even though I knew there were many bad, horribly dark days to come.

I remain convinced that the cause of my MND was largely due to certain character traits. Though feeling acute distress in times of anxiety, I tended to internalise my reactions to these stimuli.

For some reason I placed too much emphasis on the perceptions that others had of me, and I constantly needed to give the impression that I was in control in every situation, especially in my professional life. I believe that my nervous system gradually succumbed to this and, as early as 1996, began to shut down. This is precisely how my body felt - as though electricity was coursing through it and short-circuiting my nerves.

I was at my worst when being watched by someone, or among people I didn't know. I was self-conscious when people helped me or when I was being pushed around the shopping centre. I couldn't help it but hate this part of myself.

However, my self-consciousness about the impact MND was having on me didn't take away from the pride I felt in all I had accomplished in my professional life. I'd put myself through hell in my quest to carve out a career. Maybe others would have been content to sit idly by and not push themselves out of their comfort zone, but I confronted my fear and rose above it.

Optimism, according to the Encarta English dictionary, is 'the tendency to believe, expect, or hope that things will turn out well.' Maybe I will succumb to this disease, I thought, but until then I was still able to live life between my ears - I could imagine, wonder, celebrate, consider, understand, think, feel, sense, judge, and dream. For example, when I watched Eliza at play, something wonderful happened. I saw her bliss, her beautiful childish innocence and I too was immersed in the joy of the moment - it warmed my heart. Something within me leapt. She loves me unconditionally and completely, MND and all.

When I saw Lee happy and content, so too was I. When in the company of friends and family I felt the warmth of their love. At night, memories of good times past always brought a smile.

Where there's optimism, hope reigns. Hope that today I may feel better than yesterday and, if not, there's always tomorrow. Hope that my God will look upon me and smile. Hope that those near and dear to me will sustain me. Hope that I could beat this cursed disease. And hope that if not, I could find the strength to cope and actually bring some goodness to the world. I don't mean hope in terms of yearning for something. I mean hope in the sense of expectation that things will turn out well – a faith in a greater power than me.

I was never really of the belief that I would actually die from this disease. Right from the outset I felt that that I had its measure. I suppose this is true of most people's response to their own mortality – disbelief and not wanting to accept the unacceptable. The occupational therapist who visited our home in the early days when I was capable of nearly everything stated that – because of my upbeat attitude - I was clearly in denial. Needless to say, that was like a red rag to a bull for Lee and I, and though we begrudgingly listened to the rest of what she had to say, we gleefully showed her the door soon after.

My mantra was, and still is, "optimism and hope". I said it all the time and not in defeatist terms either, in the sense that I had nothing to live for and was bereft of ideas. Rather, I was starting to live it in deed and word. Let's face it, I had nothing to lose and there was so much to gain from adopting this approach. I was no longer living life just in the moment but making plans for the future. So much in life is beyond our control but not our ability to make choices regarding how we counter those events. I had said before that I fervently believed this to be true.

We can choose how we respond to certain situations and challenges, whether we cope or complain and give to life or take from life.

I could be happy or sad.

Life can be a chore or a challenge.

Ultimately, it was my choice.

I looked forward to new beginnings and a different life. Every night before I went to sleep, I visualised myself running, surfing, picking up Eliza, or just simply doing everyday chores like washing the dishes. If anybody believed I was in denial, I didn't care and I never have. What was important was adopting a positive mindset, because I had so much to live for and so many people depended on me.

I had had many affirming experiences, too many to write in these pages, but suffice to say that each one reinforced the value of relationships and how genuinely good most people are when confronted by the suffering of others. These experiences gave me cause to reflect upon my own life, my relationships, my values and the things that are important.

My own family have been extraordinary. There are not enough words to describe the love and support they constantly provide.

I wrote only briefly earlier about my sister, Donna. She is my one and only sister and we used to share a room together as kids. She has a wonderful family of four kids and a very caring husband by the name of Geoff. Donna has a genuinely good heart and still finds time to drop by and massage my hands and shoulders, even though she works full-time and always has a household of kids. Lee always knew that Donna had dropped in by the flowers that adorned the dining table that she invariably brought. I love her, not that I tell her very often, and I wonder if she knows how much she means to me. It's a thing we Andersons aren't very good at. I guess it's because we are so alpha male and tend to hide our feelings toward one another.

I will also be forever indebted to our many friends who have become family to Lee, Eliza and I. Our dear friends Mark and Lynne Evans and Michael and Megan Poulton found a way for us to buy a vehicle that holds a wheelchair - a brand new Renault. That and 23,000 odd dollars thrown in by my father and mother-in-law. We have since paid that back. They brokered a deal which saw us driving away in a new vehicle. It was actually my father-in-law, Kevin, who did the bulk of the leg-work. It has made a real difference to our life.

Some people make jokes about their in-laws but I can honestly say that I have been blessed. I have been blessed by a great family of the quality I could only dream of. Kevin and Maureen have raised a wonderful family and they should be very satisfied. They make me feel as though I belong and I love them as though they were my own. They can't do enough for me and Kev keeps mowing the lawn and doing the gardening at 75 which is no mean feat. He's a young 75 anyway, and can't do enough for us. He's always coming around and helping to make things easier for us. Maureen always has a meal ready at the drop of a hat. She seems to know intuitively what is required, and will wind up on our doorstep with whatever we need.

I never could have imagined the profound impact the Wells family would have on me. Kevin and Maureen, you took me into your loving embrace and there I have stayed. You must be so proud of your family, as such beautiful creations come about by design, not accident. I always look forward to family gatherings for their warmth, openness and laughter. I love the way hugs and kisses abound, how we sing *Happy Birthday*, and how the girls giggle like naughty schoolchildren when they're together. I love the way I can make fun at someone's expense without recriminations. I love the welcoming tenderness in their homes – all of them. But most of all, I love that they make me feel loved.

I often wondered if the tables were turned and a family member or friend was afflicted with this illness, how responsive would I be? How understanding of their needs? How ready to drop everything and run to their aid? How much of my own time would I unconditionally forego to pitch in and help with things such as painting, working bees, meals, visits, excursions to the movies, looking after their kids, organising fund raising, or going to their house after midnight to help when they have fallen? Since I had been rudely awakened to life's absolute reality, I was certainly far more confident of my answer to these questions.

I also took some consolation in the fact that I must not have been all that terrible a brother, son and mate because these people continued to love me, and cared about me and my beloved family. Above all, I was forever indebted to Lee for showing me how to reach out to others and engage them. Yes, I was far more contented in my own skin and that was a wonderful gift. My mind was clear, my demons were exorcised and I was happy with who and what I had become. I realised that my capacity as a human being and my happiness had little to do with how well I swung a golf club, what car I drove or the job title I held.

There is no textbook on how to deal with MND. This was my way and for others it may be totally different. I hoped those others have been fortunate enough along the way to experience many of the riches that I had.

Ralph Waldo Emerson, the American author, poet and philosopher expressed it so well:

> *To laugh often and love much;*
> *To win the respect of intelligent people*
> *And the affection of children;*
> *To earn the approbation of honest critics*
> *And endure the betrayal of false friends;*
> *To appreciate beauty;*
> *To find the best in others;*
> *To leave the world a bit better, whether by*
> *A healthy child, a garden patch*
> *Or a redeemed social condition;*
> *To know even one life has breathed*
> *Easier because you have lived;*
> *This is to have succeeded.*

CHAPTER 26

10 YEARS AND COUNTING

2011

I HAVEN'T UTTERED a word in nearly six years. I haven't written in four. Perhaps the hardest, most excruciating thing is my inability to communicate on even the most fundamental level. It sits like a crushing weight on us. The whole family feels it and I am so guilt-ridden. The people near and dear to me do not deserve this and it cuts me up. This ghastly disease has worn us all down, but Lee more than anyone. I am not blinded by her seemingly staunch exterior though and still see her terribly dark moments.

Lee works full-time now and has done so for the past three years. I get so lonely here at home with only the constant band of carers to keep me company over the long, drawn out days and the occasional visitor who enters through the always-open back door. Lee is an exceptional teacher and loves every minute of her work but I can't help but miss her. I am always best when Lee and Eliza are around; there's not too much to do at home without them. When Lee arrives home from school, usually around 6pm, I am well and truly sick of my own company and sick of the carers who spend the days keeping me safe and toileting me. It's nothing personal, I am fiercely independent and they're a caring bunch, but I still crave my autonomy and feel acutely my loss of it.

I now share my days primarily with my carers, who visit in four shifts every weekday with the task of putting me to bed and toileting me. Lee does the honours on the weekend. Louise and Mina are my preferred carers and do an exceptional job. They are completely different personalities, with Louise being the type to talk my ear off and Mina a quiet and happy person. I say my favourite carers for they are caring and kind and by far the most competent at what they do. It's a thankless task looking after a verbally challenged individual and I hope they know how much I appreciate their care.

I am going into respite fortnightly at present, which is a good break for Lee and Eliza. I am blessed to have happened along a great respite place at VASS, the Ventilator Accommodation Support Service. I say 'happened' because it was more luck than good management. I was at Bethlehem Hospital for my check up when a respiratory nurse mentioned such a place existed. The staff, ably led by John Puttyfoot and Ruth Crespin, provide a brilliant service and Lee and Eliza are thankful for the break. Everyone at VASS is wonderful and caring and sometimes I wonder what I would do without them. I feel very much at home there and they could not do enough for me. I miss home very much, but I do go off willingly. I regret that I need to go on a sabbatical every fortnight but do understand the reason for it.

There have been more physical symptoms and changes evident since I wrote the chapter 'Struggles and Silver Linings' almost seven years ago. I can't walk any longer (though I can still stand) and spend my days in a wheel-chair. I get so uncomfortable that sometimes I can go out of my mind, my arse screaming to shift my weight. Some people are under the misapprehension that I can't feel anything below my waist, but I feel things as keenly as I used to. It's my motor neurones that are playing up, not my sensory neurones.

I can't remember the last time I had a full night's sleep. My muscles are aching, so I'm going out of my mind. Doctors want me to put in a Baclofen pump that would sit just under my skin on my abdomen and pump a muscle relaxant through a small catheter to my spinal chord. The pump would stop the painful rigidity and spasticity in my muscles but the flipside, cruelly, is that the rigidity enables me to stand up. So I am on a full dose of Baclofen, which is as high as it can go. I won't have the pump inserted because I have lived without it for this long and feel that if I lose tone in my legs I won't be able to stand up.

If I could no longer stand, that would be the end of me. It's the only thing that separates me from the grave. It seems to give me strength to continue the battle.

Up until July 2011 I had not had any form of medical intervention. I know it sounds strange, but I felt that - if

I did – it would mean I had given up the fight. Well, obviously, I haven't given up but I've had to jump more and more hurdles to keep fighting.

I sleep in a hospital bed, which I despise. I can't remember the last time Lee and I slept together in the same bed. I miss it so, as I'm sure she does. I used to take it for granted, but now I miss it terribly.

I waged long and hard against the insertion of a PEG feed tube. I thought the only way I would have one inserted would be for Lee and Eliza not to see me slowly waste away and die a terrible death. I was warned that I'd have to have it inserted before Easter 2012 because they wouldn't put one in beyond that time – my lungs simply wouldn't hold up to the anaesthetic. As it turns out I needed to have it sooner still – August 2011 – but I am still eating a normal diet and intend to keep doing so for as long as I can.

I am also on a ventilator nightly now, but it's a major pain in the arse getting it into the right position to allow enough air in. I was getting headaches and waking up feeling less than refreshed if I had too many nights without the ventilator – my lungs no longer have capacity to fully support my breathing.

I was diagnosed about two years ago with Blepharospasm, which is a neurological condition affecting the eyes. Depending on how long they've been closed, I can't open them – no matter how hard I try. It is debilitating and distressing. I feel dreadful that my carers don't know I am trying to open my eyes to acknowledge their arrival. Once when I was in respite, a night staffer thought I was talking in my sleep, as my eyes were shut firmly – but in fact I was awake and screaming out for him to fix my pillow as it had slipped down (and my buzzer with it). Also, my eyes are extremely sensitive to light and sunglasses are a necessity when I'm in the sun. The only treatment is Botox injections in the muscles around the eyes, but this is far from pleasant and doesn't seem to have made a difference, so I've opted out.

My hands and arms are next to useless and I have problems using my LightWriter, which is my major means of communication. There is eye-activated technology available but the muscles in my eyes are so painful to move sideways, I can't use that method of communication. Instead, I 'speak' by using a laser affixed to a cap, and an alphabet board attached to my wheelchair. For every word I want to spell out, I have to point the laser at each letter, and hope the red light lands dead on the square. If the laser skews slightly towards another letter, the whole context of what I am trying to say changes, and makes it even harder for people to predict or interpret the words I am spelling out. It is a slow, trying and tedious process, requiring much patience – and spelling ability. You'd be surprised at the number of people who can't spell, even when I do get the light on the right letter! It's not that I can't move my hands, but they are so gnarled and bent, they take so long to move and require so much effort that I get very tired. I can straighten them after hours of rest, but the doctor remains worried I will grow my fingernails into my hands. I have splints to stop this from happening, and will test out whether sleeping with my hands in the splints improves movement at all.

My laughter is out of control and I usually have a

stupid grin on my face. That's not too bad, but when Eliza is doing something dangerous or naughty I can't tell her to stop because I am grinning like a cheshire cat. She often enjoys a joke at my expense and I am so busy laughing that I can't raise enough strength to retort on my LightWriter or let out a disapproving grunt.

I can no longer get food to my mouth. I can still drink through a straw, but I haven't had a beer for at least three years – and that's killing me! I can no longer feed myself, which adds an extra dimension to going out. I am consumed by embarrassment when other people feed me because I don't have the manners I used to, and food keeps finding a way of exiting my mouth and winding up on my shirt. Poor Lee can't enjoy meal times because she needs to feed me. I'm always dribbling because I have more secretions than I used to and can't swallow effectively or as often as I used to. This is very embarrassing in public. Family know to keep a cloth at the ready when we're out and about.

I am more than ever the wallflower, and I'm really struggling with this. I was at a party last week and found that nobody spoke to me. I can't say I blame them, because I don't have much to offer in a conversation. This I find intolerable and is not me at all. I tend in social situations to rely on Lee more than ever. We still go out thanks to the Renault and I love the normalcy this brings to everyday life.

However, I have had to miss taking Eliza on the longer holidays to Samoa and on many trips to Queensland. Lee and Eliza had a wonderful time in 2009 when they went to Samoa to stay with my brother Matt, who was posted over there as High Commissioner. I stayed in respite and Lee sent me updates by email and photos of their time. Eliza was snorkelling and had a great time with her cousins Meg and Kate. The next stop may be the Solomon Islands. I guess I will need to miss that too. Matt and Lou will be there through Matt's role as High Commissioner. It's so difficult not being there as Eliza encounters all that will shape her values, skills and life experiences in her formative years. I sometimes feel like the absent parent, unable to make any decisions about my own flesh and blood.

This is my third draft of this chapter. I normally don't need to draft, just tinker around the edges of a chapter until it sounds how I want it to sound. I guess the reason for so many drafts is because of the word processing program I need to use now. Dasher, rather than Word, is a mouse-activated program whereby I 'collect' letters at the bottom of the screen, and they arrange into potential word configurations – similar to predictive text - at the top of the screen. I select the word configuration that I want, and move on to making the next word. However the program is now getting too fast for me, as I often can't select the word I want in time, and so it just drops in the first option it comes up with. Hence the need to rewrite so much. I also now need someone to place my hand on the mouse as I can't unfurl my grip without assistance.

I was also informed by one of my neurologists that my writing may suffer as a result of MND and I think this has proven correct. Scientists have only recently discovered that for people with the slower progressing form of MND – the form that I have - mental capacity and organisational functional can in fact deteriorate.

I also believe my reason for so much redrafting is because I feel this cursed disease has got the better of me mentally, yet I badly want this chapter to sound more in keeping with the positive tone of the book. I have truly struggled with reconciling the reality of my present with the conviction of my past writing and experiences.

With all the symptoms and changes over the past four years since I last wrote, I was beginning to feel sorry for myself, something I rarely do, and I was beginning to use phrases like 'why me' and 'it isn't fair' in my writing. It was Lee who pointed it out to me. She said there was so much wrong with this chapter and its tone, where would I start to make it better?

Even worse, she was angry at me.

I had blamed her for being lonely here at home and held her responsible for all manner of things. I guess my reason for feeling this way stemmed from the fact that I wanted to contribute something; anything other than pain to those who I am closest to. How could I justify causing those near to me such pain and misery? More than that, I wanted to feel that I was still contributing to the greater good. Like there's a reason for our suffering that is beyond our understanding but is there nevertheless. I couldn't find it, though I had searched for meaning and asked God for strength.

At times I just couldn't find any reason to keep plodding along and, although Lee and Eliza remained the big reasons, it was difficult to justify the pain I was causing them. I sometimes couldn't help but think they'd be better if I wasn't here. I was being so negative, dark and sombre when I didn't have a right to. I have much to be thankful for, but it was getting more difficult to see through all the complications of everyday life.

However, all I really need do is look in to my gorgeous Eliza's eyes and see her beautiful radiance and the wonder that she sees in every day to recapture the incredulity and marvel of life.

Eliza and Lee are my reason for getting out of bed every day. I have written this previously, but it is so true today. Eliza is a shining light. She keeps me from getting miserable and from pitying myself. She seems unfazed by my illness, but I'm sure she isn't. Lee and I have our eyes on any changes in her behaviour and demeanour as we are incredibly mindful of what our little girl has missed out on because of MND.

Eliza is understandably anxious about any illness that affects her or people she cares about. Perhaps fearing that every ailment is serious, she will describe her own symptoms in detail to Lee, and needs lots of explanation and reassurance to be convinced everything is okay. We've read in materials produced by the various MND associations that this anxiety and preoccupation with illness is very common with kids who live with a terminal illness. Eliza also worries about something happening to her mum, once asking Lee 'Who would look after me and Dad if you weren't here?' For all that these worries may be common, it is so very hard to see our little girl grapple with such heartbreaking questions.

Eliza has been more reluctant to go away without Lee or I in recent times, which means we need to strike a very fine balance between pushing through her anxiety and understanding why she feels this way. Again, separation anxiety is common for kids like Eliza, but it's probably exacerbated by the fact that she is an only child and has no siblings to distract her from the realities of her parents' life. Lee and I are half-convinced Eliza has bionic hearing – she is incredibly tuned in to everything that is going on and chatters away to Lee the whole time in the car, asking questions where she hasn't understood or been worried by what she's heard. While we'd prefer she didn't hear so much, Lee and I are grateful for her openness and tendency to ask these questions, rather than worry away to herself.

She asked Lee last year if I was going to die before the end of the year but Lee assured her that, barring some untoward lung infection, I would be okay. She said she wants to keep my surfboard in her room. I guess she will get more use out of it than I did. I was watching her on her skateboard the other night and she's very good. If she has the same skills surfing, she'll be okay. For Christmas in 2010 we gave her a surfing lesson at Torquay and she loved it. There will be plenty more where that came from, I can tell you.

For all the worry, Eliza has grown into a caring and sensitive young girl who is always willing to look out for the needs of others. Lee and I see the positive impact that my having MND has had on Eliza, as strange as that sounds. Even at 11 she has an innate sense of compassion and is a truly good and sensitive young person. She knows she has to look out for me and has learned, without even realising it, what it's like for someone to live with a disability. Eliza will frequently point out to Lee why a particular place would be 'good' for me – she just automatically notices the ramps, lifts, exits and other facilities. She recently asked her PE teacher if I would be able to get into the venue for her school athletics; he hadn't considered it but, once asked, adjusted the event accordingly. In a science project last year, without any input or prompting from Lee or I, Eliza invented a 'auto-magnoholder' – a table on wheels with wire and magnets "to get my dad the remote." She wrote, "It can be used anywhere. Other people with disabilities can use our invention." In looking out for me, Eliza is influencing other people to look out for anyone with a disability. It makes Lee and I proud beyond words.

We are also so proud of how accepting of difference Eliza is. She is never judgmental of those with differences, difficulties or disabilities and has a remarkable ability at such a young age to explain people's behaviour as a result of those differences. Everyone around her notices her kindness and compassion. Eliza recently completed a major project for school where her classmates assessed her presentation and then gave her feedback on both her presentation and personality. Overwhelmingly, the characteristics her young peers attributed to Eliza were the very same characteristics Lee and I have observed, nurtured and wondered at over the years:

"She's kind"
"She's a good friend"
"She's always there for you"
"She has a really nice personality"
"She's beautiful in all sorts of ways"
"Eliza is really honest"

"She works really hard"

"Her wisdom"

"She's confident doing things"

"She has a go at things"

"She helps people, even if they have hurt her in the past"

"She's always so happy"

"She's never bossy"

"She never gives up"

Yes, MND has affected our daughter, but Lee and I fervently believe that the good will continue to outweigh the bad. Eliza really is a special gift and every day we thank God that we have her.

I remain in complete awe of Lee, who looks as though she is untouched by this terrible, shitty existence. Who could work full-time, unencumbered by this wretched disease, with countless nights of interrupted sleep, fronting up to work seemingly unscathed by the activities of the night before? Who could show up looking like she's straight out of a glamorous fashion model magazine? Yes, I happened on a real good one there.

And I am especially proud of the way I have continued to smile my way through this life sentence… all the way through to what, I concede, will be my death.

I have not given up on life, just grasped the reality of my present.

CHAPTER 27

UNPLANNED ROAD
by Leanne Anderson

I FIRST MET Pete just over 21 years ago. It was back in 1990 when I started my teaching career at Mount Lilydale College. Like Pete, I was summonsed by Sister Beth to her office at the end of my last teaching round and asked if I would be interested in taking up a full time position at the college the following year. As you can imagine I was ecstatic, as I hadn't yet graduated and therefore accepted the position of being part of the Year 7 Homeroom team on the spot. I remember accepting the appointment with both excitement and apprehension at the fact I would be returning to the school as both a qualified teacher and an old Collegian.

Little did I know in accepting the position, I was about to embark upon some of the happiest memories of my career as an educator and meet the man I would choose to marry.

I was in a relationship when I started at Mount Lilydale

College, so apart from being extremely conscientious and diligent as a first year out teacher, I had no inclination to be searching for a companion of the male kind. However, like I always do when I am in a new environment, I observe and get a feel for what the place and the people are like. It is not in my personality to throw myself into a situation without caution and serious consideration. In other words, I am far from spontaneous. I am a strong believer that prevention is better than cure.

Needless to say, although I was physically attracted to Pete from our early encounters, I needed to witness for myself that he was decent and treated people well. It took very little time before I summed him up as being extremely decent and extremely everything you could want in a person. It was at this point I made the decision to end the relationship I was in. Amazing how word got around because a week later Pete asked me out. The memory of our first date at Whispers in Balwyn is one of gourmet food, good wine, interesting conversation and lots of laughter. I also caught a glimpse of Pete's romantic side as he handed me a beautiful bouquet of flowers on my arrival. To this day, after twenty-one years of being together and sixteen years of marriage I sometimes arrive home from work to find flowers on the doorstep awaiting me. Lucky for online shopping!

Even though I was five years younger than Pete it all just felt right. I could tell from day one that we both shared so many similarities in our upbringings, our values and even our personalities. We loved to socialise with family and friends, we loved to experience new adventures and we loved doing things together. In summary, we loved life. Qualities that also shone through with Pete from day one were his understanding of people and an innate desire to help others. I also remember that although Pete was oblivious to what life would throw at us as a little later, he taught me how to put things in perspective. If I was ever upset Pete would in his calm but caring manner suggest I put my worry or concern on a scale of 1-10. It's quite ironic that 10 was always that a loved one had been told they have a terminal illness. As you can imagine, many of my worries at the time were not worth putting on the continuum.

After much speculation from family and friends of when and where the proposal would happen, Pete and I were engaged in the August of 1994. It was a Friday night and we had just finished a meal at one of our favourite Vietnamese restaurants in Canterbury called Phon's when Pete suggested we head into the city and take a look at the view from the top of the Rialto building. It was here overlooking Melbourne that Pete asked me to marry him. We had been together for five years prior to this so felt we were ready to make the commitment to spending our lives together. Although we didn't live together before marrying we had travelled with each other, including a seven week whirlwind trip to various parts of the world. Even though we were not officially part of an *Amazing Race* series, my documentation of the trip indicates we did 27 different flights on this journey. We both came to the conclusion that if we could survive this, we could survive living together.

Pete and I married in the following April. A simple, relaxed yet extremely joyous occasion.

The day I got married was definitely up there with the highlights of my life. Not so much for the event itself, but because I felt truly blessed that I had found this wonderful man who I had no doubt would look after me and love me for the rest of my life. I remember clearly that I was not nervous or anxious about the commitment I was making on that day. I knew Pete Anderson was the man for me. I guess what I didn't realise was that when I confidently proclaimed our vows, 'For better, for worse, in sickness and in health, until death do us part', I would be truly challenged in living these out.

It was on 21 June 2001, on a cold Thursday evening, that this challenge began. It was on this evening that we as a young couple, just starting our family, were told that Pete had been diagnosed with MND. When we first received this devastating news Pete and I dealt with it the way we normally approached hardships. It was a problem to be fixed so we needed to start looking at ways of how we could do this. A little naive I guess, but determined that with a positive attitude and support from family and friends we would be ok and we would win this battle. I could never have imagined the complexities of living with such an illness and the impact it would have on every aspect of our lives. We had to come to terms with the fact that no matter how hard we tried we could not escape the reality of how MND would eventually ravage every part of Pete's body and would ultimately dictate his last breath.

Once we digested these cold, hard facts we started to move towards reading about management of the different symptoms Pete would encounter. We uncovered stories of other families who had been forced to endure a similar road. I remember my sister Melissa, who at the time was living in New York assisting us in our quest for answers. She sent me a story of a couple who had fought the battle of MND for eight long years. The revelations from this story have long stayed with me. I clearly remember reading that as time passed the woman had been forced to adjust to the fact that the relationship they shared had moved from husband and wife to nurse and patient. At the time this was something I came to dread. Pete and I had always shared a close, open and fun-filled relationship based on mutual respect and equality. I never envisaged it would be anything else.

How could I ever have foreseen how brutal this insidious disease would be on our relationship? It is excruciatingly painful to watch the person who is closest to you, your best friend, your husband, the person you have chosen to be your life-long partner and the person you love unconditionally slowly disappearing before your eyes. The grieving process is gradual because, although the losses are not sudden, they are happening.

I admire Pete so much for the dignity and spirit he has shown in his daily battle against MND. It truly astounds me that someone who has had to suffer so much can still be content with his life. In this way Pete shines through the MND, which perhaps explains why those of our friends who didn't know him pre-MND still truly 'get' his personality, even though they've only known him to be ill. They've just taken it all on board and see beyond Pete's illness, finding ways to include him. I find this incredible. Pete still loves socialising despite the limitations he faces and I have no doubt that I would not have coped the way I have if Pete's personality had turned dark and morose. I guess that's why I was a little disappointed when I read Pete's original piece about where we are at now on this journey, because even though we go through tough periods, 'depressed' or 'beaten' are not two words I would use to define Peter Anderson. I recognise it is Pete's qualities of strength, determination, tolerance and calmness that have enabled him to maintain quality of life. Of course, this is not saying Pete does not have bad days. In fact there are days when the idea of ending the battle torments his mind.

Often people who only see Pete periodically will comment on how well he is looking and that there doesn't appear to have been much deterioration. When people visit our home, Pete is usually sitting laconically in his electric wheelchair, looking dapper in his surfy-labelled clothes with a big smile plastered across his face. I fully understand these observations because the changes that are taking place in Pete's body are very subtle to the untrained and objective eye. Although it is not obvious when friends visit, so much is happening in Pete's daily struggle behind the smile.

For sufferers of MND, the actions of walking, talking and feeding are covertly stolen, one after the other. Each time this occurs it is with a sense of grief and loss for what once was. One day you can walk and the next you are confined to a wheelchair. One day you can freely talk and the next your mouth struggles to form the words until finally it is impossible to express even your basic needs. One day you can eat by yourself and the next you are dependent on others to feed you. I can clearly remember the morning Pete could no longer tie his own shoelaces and shortly after that, he wasn't able to put shoes or socks on by himself. I clearly remember the day when he couldn't lift his arms above his head, so he could no longer wash his hair. Then Pete could no longer lift his hands to his mouth, so he couldn't feed himself nor could he clean his own teeth. Unlike most other things in my life, I am powerless over these changes and feel incredibly helpless and heartbroken at not being able to make things better.

There are many things I miss about Pete. I miss communicating with him where tone, inflection and expression provide meaning. I miss having an inbuilt companion to talk to at home about anything and everything. I used to love it when he would arrive home from work and we would sit and have a coffee while unravelling the events of the day or make a start on tea and have a chat while doing so. We had this unwritten rule that whoever cooked, the other would clean up afterwards. I think I am fair in saying I was the better cook so Pete probably washed a few more dishes than me. Pete did try hard to broaden his culinary talents although he was a stickler for following a recipe, so would be completely thrown if we didn't have one of the ingredients in the pantry.

I particularly miss being able to casually share our thoughts about Eliza. Pete's words of wisdom can no longer be given and deliberations no longer mulled over. It's not quite the same when you have to send an email from work about matters of concern and wait for the following day to receive a response. Nor is it the same to have

Pete make one-word requests through his LightWriter. Even though I am fully aware it is not Pete's fault and he has to economise with words, it is still nicer to hear 'Can I please have a coffee?' rather than just 'Coffee'. I must admit though, he has typed some very funny things into this clever little machine and he finds great joy in typing things like 'You idiot' when I do or say something ridiculous. This makes me laugh because I can always imagine him actually saying this to me and the tone that he would be using if he could talk.

His voice is what I miss the most out of everything.

Pete is now the silent spectator in his own life. One of the things that hurts him the most is that he can no longer involve himself actively with Eliza, our beautiful daughter. Eliza is now eleven years of age and as she was only twelve months old when Pete was diagnosed with MND, she has known no different. Eliza adores Pete and loves him unconditionally. There is no doubt that she gets sad about Pete's inability to do certain things and there is definitely a level of frustration there at having to sometimes play the role of carer to her Mum and Dad. I cannot blame her at times for getting annoyed when I ask her to get Pete a drink or pass him the remote. These seem like small tasks but ones your parents can normally do independently, yet are tasks you have to do on a daily basis when your Dad has MND. However, I know these rudimentary tasks will fade into insignificance.

For her, it is having Dad sit on the sidelines every Saturday morning at Vermont South Netball Stadium watching every move she makes. It is having Dad at events like her birthday parties, the Father's Day Breakfast at school, her First Eucharist, and her school music concert, amidst many others, that mean the most to her. I always have the camera on hand to capture these memories as this is what matters.

One day last year when Eliza came home from school she proceeded to recount the events of her lunchtime. She started by telling Pete and I she had played cricket. I noticed how Pete's face lit up at this news. During the match Eliza was told by the other kids that she was out because her bat hit the wickets. I looked at Pete's face. She went on to say she had no idea that was a rule and at the time was prepared to go out even after her friends offered her another go. Despite feeling injustice at not knowing the rules of the game, in true Peter Anderson style she walked.

I could tell by Pete's expression he was proud. He was always a stickler for kids playing by the rules. There were never any second chances with Pete as umpire. If you were out, you were out. For me this moment symbolised a number of irreversible truths.

Eliza, unlike other kids, had grown up without games of backyard cricket with her dad and this is why she was not aware of that rule. The opportunity to teach Eliza the rules of the game he loved had been taken away from Pete. And for me it was another unexpected cost of this disease, yet another unforseen pitfall on the journey. As our lives unfolded, it was becoming increasingly apparent that there are many parenting gaps I would have to fill on my own. This was not part of our plan.

This is one of the hardest aspects for me. Although we are still alongside each other, I often feel as if I am parenting alone. We were always such a good team and approached everything together but now one of our players is seriously injured. Despite trying our best we cannot shoot or kick as many goals. I know Pete has a feeling of missing out when we go away and this is another area I need to be mindful of managing. I don't want Eliza to miss out on experiences but I don't want Pete to feel excluded either – and it would be better for me if he was there able-bodied. As much as it pains me for Pete not to be involved in everything I do with Eliza, the reality is he is very ill; there are limitations on what we can do as a family and what I can manage.

One vivid memory I have was when I was putting Eliza to bed one night. Pete had growled at her earlier in the evening over a tantrum she was having. Although he couldn't speak the words he wanted, he made a very loud and disapproving noise which clearly sent the message to Eliza that he was not happy with her behaviour. Eliza proceeded to tell me that because Dad was sick she didn't think he would have feelings. She thought he would lose the ability to be angry, sad, happy and so on. She used the *Wizard of Oz* to help explain what she meant by saying that the Tin Man couldn't feel because he didn't have a heart. Holding back my own tears, I reassured her that no matter how sick Dad gets, he would always have feelings, just like us. If only things were pre-MND. I know that when Eliza is being argumentative or difficult for me or when she is feeling cross or upset, all it would take would be a firm or comforting word from her father.

I also know that because of our personalities, we have different things to offer. It saddens me that Pete is not able to play around and have a joke with Eliza because he is much better at making light of things than me. Eliza possesses a great sense of humour and has an ability to pick the perfect moment to come out with some great one-liners. In those moments I see Pete. Even when she was in Prep, her first year of primary school, she would come home from school and tell me that some of the boys were mucking around but they were actually very funny. However, she had to 'laugh in her head' because otherwise she would get in trouble.

As much as I hate to admit it, Pete would probably score higher in the general knowledge stakes than I would. This means that when Eliza asks those inquisitive questions, my response is, 'I think you'll have to Google that one sweetie.' Although Peter is very much still with us, the ability to impart his knowledge in these situations has been stolen and we are the poorer for it.

Deep down I also believe that Eliza would not experience the same level of anxiety as she does if Pete were well. Her primary burden is for Pete's wellbeing but at times her fears are revealed in other ways. I'm assuming she would not be as petrified of dogs because I'm sure Pete would have wangled a golden retriever into our family by now.

I guess she is a reflection of both of us. I see how loyal she is to family and friends and how she is always concerned about the needs of others. Even at her young age she has this amazing ability to empathise. Seeing her display these qualities always makes me feel proud of who she is and the person she is becoming. Although it hurts me when I think of the things Eliza has missed out on as a result of living with MND, I do think we owe ourselves some credit for the positive way in which we have tackled this challenge. In any decision Pete and I make we always have Eliza's wellbeing at the forefront of our minds.

I have been asked on a number of occasions whether I regret making the decision not to have more children after Pete's diagnosis. I regret that I have not been able to have more children as I had always hoped to have three and I know the joy it would bring Eliza to have a brother or sister. However, I still believe Pete and I made the right decision at the time we made it. When we received the news in 2001 that Pete could have as little as three years life expectancy, we did not feel it was right to bring a child into the world knowing they may have very little or no time with their father. In hindsight we had plenty of time but no one could have predicted this. We do not dwell on this as we consider ourselves very lucky to have our daughter Eliza.

Throughout Eliza's childhood we have endeavoured to make her days as 'normal' as possible. She is a very social little girl and like her Mum and Dad loves the company of friends and family. Eliza certainly likes an event. The planning, enthusiasm and excitement that goes into organising birthdays and other celebrations by Eliza is extremely uplifting for Pete and I because it is a sign of her ability to enjoy the good times amidst the hardships. Like most other children she has tried different activities. Up to this point she has done dancing, piano, netball and tennis. She is still doing netball and tennis which she loves and wants to have a go at learning the guitar and singing lessons. I love the way she'll give most things a go.

Like for us, it has been a journey for Eliza. Along the way she has asked me all sorts of questions. When she was four or five she had moved on from making observations about Pete's physical deterioration and wanted to know all about what it was like in heaven. I remember her asking me if you lie down or stand up and she also wanted to know if your eyes are open or shut and whether there are toilets in heaven. I can't remember exactly how I answered these questions but they were certainly curly ones and probably an early indication of her being a deep thinker.

Our brave little daughter then stunned me on another occasion when I was driving along and she asked from the back seat whether the doctors had found a medicine yet that would fix Dad. Pete and I had always been very honest with Eliza in telling her that Dad would only get better if a cure was found for MND. I tried to provide an answer that was true but would not encourage false hope. I told her that the scientists and researchers are working very hard to try and find a cure but are yet to find one. This wasn't enough for her though. She proceeded to ask how the researchers could be sure that the medicine would work. I replied that lots of tests are done on animals before they trial it on humans. Like always, she had to have the last say and queried how this could be possible when humans are so different to animals.

We have now reached a point where Eliza has come to the realisation that Pete's illness eventually leads to death. She is only 11 years old and I so wish that she didn't have to carry this burden with her every day. It was the middle of last year, 2010, and she asked me if there was any chance Dad could die before the end of the year. I told her that it was very unlikely because of the slow progression of MND in Pete but nor could I promise that it wouldn't because if Pete were to get a nasty chest infection it could be a grave concern. Her response was one that I wasn't ready for. She asked if she would be able to keep Pete's things if he did die, in particular his surfboard. I was able to promise her then that she could keep anything she wanted. Needless to say that was another evening I left her room sobbing, having kissed her and tucked her into bed.

Holiday adventures have always been important to Pete and I and we have endeavoured to provide the same sorts of experiences for Eliza as we had as children. In her early life we had a couple of trips to Queensland with our good friends the Evans and the Poultons, whereby she would spend many an hour swimming either in the surf or in the pool at Lynne's aunty's place in Broadbeach. Eliza also treasures our holidays to Port Fairy, Mount Martha and Phillip Island with our dear friends the McKennas and although it always seems to rain on our holidays together, there is never a shortage of laughter and good times. No matter how we are feeling, Marty and Jac have this amazing ability to cheer us up and keep our spirits high, despite the fact that many of Marty's jokes are at my expense. Eliza and I were also very lucky to have the opportunity in 2009 to visit Pete's brother Matt and his family in Samoa. To see Eliza jumping off rocks, snorkelling and feeding turtles brought tears to my eyes. At this time and in this place she was allowed to be the innocent and unburdened child she was entitled to be. Relaxed and happy.

In September 2010 we also managed to get away but this time as a whole family, thanks to the support of my wonderful Mum and Dad. It had been about two years since we had all been away together, something Eliza longs for, and so I asked my parents if they would be happy to spend a week with us in Bright. I think this trip was a perfect example of how hard it is as a mum in this situation to be meeting the needs of all the family. I could see how important it was for Pete to get away and witness the joy Eliza experiences on holidays. As a person who now has to spend most weekdays within the confines of our home he was also desperate for a change of scenery. I knew deep down though the trip was not going to be easy, from either a logistical or nursing point of view. If Pete was to come with us we would have to transport all of his equipment, including electric wheelchair, manual wheelchair, commode, hoist, ventilator and several other bits and pieces. Luckily Dad has a trailer, so we loaded everything on and off we went.

Eliza's close friend Ella Beveridge from Kilmore also came on the trip with us. Thanks to Mum and Dad the girls were able to stay in their cabin, which meant they were not affected by the sleepless nights Pete and I encountered, nor the other mishaps that unfolded.

I am not used to sleeping in the same room as Pete and was therefore not used to the constant moaning and groaning sounds that interrupt the silence of the night. The problem was that every time I heard him I would jump up and turn the light on, only to find he was actually asleep. Then there would be the times when he was consciously groaning as he needed my assistance for toileting. I was only telling my family the other day that I am nice at the 11pm call, reasonable at the 2am call and then not so pleasant at the 4.30am call. I know we all do this when our children are babies but you don't anticipate you will be nursing your husband in this capacity in the middle years of your life.

Although I found this part of the trip taxing, it was reassuring that the two girls were oblivious to the hardships as Mum and Dad had them off trout fishing, walking, bike riding, swimming in the river, buying ice creams and tobogganing at Mount Hotham. Pete was very keen to witness the girls tobogganing so we all went to Mount Hotham. But of all places for me to forget Pete's urinal bottle, Mount Hotham probably wasn't the pick. Due to the extreme temperatures, Pete was unable to get out of our van. Instead, we had to find a car park whereby he could view the girls sliding down the slopes. Another example of Pete being forced to play the spectator. Anyway, just before we were about to head home, Pete indicated he needed to go to the toilet. It was at this point I realised I did not have the bottle and we were therefore in real strife. Dad and I started rummaging through our cars, while Mum was pouring the girls a hot chocolate, to see if we could find a suitable substitute. I must say my eyes lit up when Dad pulled out the chamois holder. I proceeded to do what you have to do when you are helping your husband aim into a chamois holder while he remains seated in his wheelchair inside the car. Believe me, it is awkward! All seemed to be going as planned when I noticed a telltale wet patch on Pete's jeans. Suddenly both Pete and the car were flooded! Unfortunately neither Dad nor I had noticed the tiny hole in the bottom of the chamois holder.

I look back at this situation now and laugh but at the time it wasn't funny because such accidents seem to happen with monotonous regularity. What it did mean was that Pete's trip back to Bright was extremely uncomfortable and my thoughts were of the laborious task of changing him when we got home. This kind of tainted my view of the snow-capped mountains that surrounded me as I drove back. Once again, Eliza and Ella were protected from the knowledge of this drama as Nanna Maureen, as always, did a fantastic job distracting them.

This story is worth recounting because these are the daily inconveniences and hiccups we face as a family. No matter how positive we are and how eager we are to have normal family experiences, there is no denying that any outing is arduous, problematic and exhausting. Having said this I will always treasure the happy memories of this trip and not focus on the inconvenient mishaps. I am reminded and reassured by the photos because it was a time when we were all together as a complete family. As the progression of MND continues in Pete, I never know if we will get to go on such a holiday again.

Eliza and I set off on another adventure in April 2011. This time we did a road trip to check out all that Canberra has to offer, with Eliza's cousin Taylah (her adopted big sister). As with all the trips we do without Pete, a focus of our time was selecting a suitable souvenir especially chosen by Eliza. Of course, we also take many photos to add to the family collection. We all know this cannot take the place of him being there but it does mean that he is momentarily present on our holiday, just the same.

So now to the question I am frequently asked and that is, 'How do you cope?' I think I cope because I have an amazing network of friends and family and I am surrounded by so much good. I could actually write a whole book on the acts of generosity that have come our way throughout our journey. In the early days I may have expected close friends and family to reach out in our time of need, but to think ten years down the track the same people are by our side helping out in any way they possibly can is extraordinary. Pete has already mentioned some of the big events that have been organised in our honour and as much as these have enabled us to extend our house and purchase a wheelchair friendly vehicle, it is the day-to-day support that helps to lighten my load.

It is Jo Ginnane, Pete's cousin arriving every Friday afternoon with a beautiful meal for us. Jo has been doing this for close to nine years now and if ever she is not able to make it on the Friday she will ensure she drops in on the Thursday or Saturday. I find this commitment from a person who leads an extremely full and busy life remarkable. It is my sister Karen who, when I made the decision in the early days of Pete's diagnosis to return to work, offered to look after Eliza. At this stage Karen had all four of her children off at school yet sacrificed having time on her own to help me out. It is Pete's sister, Donna, who when I returned to work would come over and clean my house. I always knew she had been because a bunch of long stemmed roses was strategically arranged in a vase on our dining room table. Another mother of four who I am sure had more pleasurable activities she could have been doing.

It is our friends, Mark and Lynne, who amidst demanding work commitments and raising three active children, still manage to schedule a monthly get together whereby we share some Asian takeaway which they pick up on their way in. Lynne and I always manage to crack open a bottle of champagne to accompany our meal and enjoy the fact that neither of us have to cook. It is my loyal and dear friend, Marita, who lovingly looks after Eliza before and after school. Reat is always there for me and never makes me feel guilty for the fact that I cannot repay her for the ongoing support she has given me. I love our chats over a glass of wine. Whenever I speak to Reat I feel like she really listens to me and always gives me the impression she understands what I am going through.

It is my friend of thirty-five years, Fi, who is constantly seeking out ways to help. Despite the fact that a couple of months can go past without seeing each other she is always texting or ringing purely to ask if we are all doing ok. Remarkable considering Fi and Nick have had their own family concerns with their son Patrick being diagnosed with diabetes just over twelve months ago.

It is our friend, Steve Palmer, sacrificing four days of his annual holiday to paint our deck and in doing so, making it seem like no big deal.

It is Pete's mum, Margaret, who remains a pillar of strength for us both. She is a remarkable woman and I am forever indebted to her for the support she has given us.

I have only mentioned a few but there have been countless acts of kindness directed our way.

I have certainly had to make changes to my life as a result of Pete's illness. I have become more flexible and have had to adapt to the fact that no matter how organised you are things can go wrong. As a person who always liked things to be spot on I have had to let go here. My house is no longer immaculate but I have discovered there are more important things to worry about. I have grown to appreciate that it is the basic pleasures that are most important in life.

When Pete is in respite, which, as of the beginning of this year is Monday to Friday every fortnight, I do not have this burning desire to be out on the town making the most of my freedom. Instead, I savour the moment of being able to eat my meals without feeding Pete at the same time. I love getting into bed at night knowing I will not be awakened by the ding dong of Pete's buzzer. I love getting up in the morning and making a cup of coffee without first toileting Pete. I love arriving home after work to find everything in exactly the same place. I love lying on Eliza's bed reading to her knowing that we won't be interrupted by the doorbell, the indicator that Pete's evening carer has arrived to put him into bed. I guess these are all things I took for granted prior to living with MND.

My work also helps to sustain me. As much as it can be extremely stressful at times, it fulfils me and provides me with purpose. I truly love working with young people. Although I am meant to be the teacher, I learn so much from them and gain great energy from my involvement with the students I teach.

Amidst the strain and heartache that MND places on

the relationship Pete and I share, the wonderful thing is that I can still talk openly and honestly to him. I know it is still the Pete I first met twenty-one years ago that lies within the frail body. Although he can't comfort me the way he used to by embracing me or by imparting words of empathy, he still looks at me with understanding in his eyes and will give a gentle raise of the thumb to say "I get it".

We will continue to run the marathon with our support crew, no doubt stumbling on the rocks in our path. While doing so, I hope we will always be able to absorb the goodness that life has to offer. To focus on what we have rather than what we think we want or don't have. There are so many people in this world who are far worse off than us as they exist with a feeling that no one loves them and no one cares.

Twenty years ago I never imagined I would be sitting here, writing this story. It was not the story I imagined for Pete, for Eliza, for me. This predicament we have found ourselves in is unexpected and unimaginable. It has certainly been an endurance test for the three of us, a daily challenge that demands so much. Qualities have emerged in each of us which have resourced us as we accept and confront these challenges. We now know that we have the capacity to live our lives with hope. We are equipped to navigate what is sure to be an even more difficult road ahead. We have proven that our love for each other is greater than all that resists and threatens to keep it strong.

FOR ELIZA MAY

"YOU ARE A TREASURE, A BLESSING, A PRAYER'S ANSWER"
Gabriel Byrne

Mum was being rushed into theatre for an emergency caesarean section. For more than four hours we watched the foetal monitor dip from 135 beats per minute down to as low as 78. In stark contrast, my heart was beating through my chest wall. The midwives at Mitcham Private Hospital were concerned. They did not say as much, but I could tell by their sideways glances that all was not going according to plan. You were struggling and in distress; so were we. Every time your heart rate plunged, so too did our spirits. We held our breath until it returned to normal, only to watch it drop time and time again. Where is the obstetrician? Can't someone do something? Finally he arrives and takes charge. He reads the data from the monitor and immediately decides to go the caesarean route. 'I am not asking you, I am telling you - that's what we have to do', he says. Who are we to argue? As Mum was being prepped and I was putting on my theatre scrubs, I was impressed and reassured by the calmness and professionalism of the doctors and nurses present.

It's a girl! All scrawny and shrivelled up, not at all like the radiant beauty you soon turned out to be. The doctor called you 'Thorpey' because you had such long, skinny feet – we preferred Eliza May. I immediately adored all 3004 grams and 51 centimetres of you. While Mum was being stitched up, a midwife took a photograph of me timidly clutching my new baby daughter – it remains one of my most cherished possessions. You know the one because you love it too. It's in your album. I also love the photo of the first time I gave you a bath in the hospital nursery. You enjoyed the warm water lapping at your skin. As you grew from a toddler to a child you would take long baths and I would sit in the doorway, watching you splash and play games. Remember how we would give Mum a surprise when you hopped out, dried yourself and got into your pyjamas? You were so pleased with yourself and I was so proud. Mum pretended she didn't know what was going on and when you'd appear all dressed she went into raptures telling you how big and grown up you had become.

When we brought you home from hospital, Mum and I were quite nervous. We need not have been for you were the perfect baby, very placid, sedate and quiet. Mum had set up your bedroom beautifully with a gorgeous white cradle that would rock you off to sleep. In the morning we'd bring you into our bed for a play – you brought us so much joy. Sometimes you would lie face down on my chest and I'd give you the biggest cuddles. I loved the sweet smell of your hair and skin, that baby smell of mild soap and powder. Even now when you sit on my knee I sneakily bury my nose in your hair to catch the gentle fragrance. When you were four weeks old I broke my leg whilst going for a run and had to go to hospital to have it pinned – the same hospital in which you were born. Unfortunately I couldn't help Mum very much, but I was still able to nurse you.

As you grew we started taking you on holidays to our favourite places; Sorrento, Queensland, Adelaide and beyond. You loved playing at the beach, which warmed my heart because that is my favourite place too. I had visions of you riding next to me on the same wave, laughing excitedly as we weaved our way to shore. You received your first wipe-out as a baby at Torquay, when I left you sitting on the sand at my feet. Marty and I were talking when a large wave came in and swept you off your bottom, sending you rolling end over end down into the rushing water. You coughed and spluttered a few times but otherwise you were fine. We had many wonderful times on our holidays but, as time marched relentlessly forward, I couldn't play with you as I used to. It was extremely difficult to see other dads pulling you around on your boogey board and making sand castles with you, but your laughter and sheer enjoyment mollified my self-indulgent feelings of inadequacy.

When you were 13 months old I was diagnosed with Motor Neurone Disease. Mum and I had always planned on giving you one or two brothers and/or sisters but unfortunately had to make the excruciating decision to stop after we had you. There were many complex reasons that led to our decision. First and foremost in our minds was the extremely negative prognosis we received from the doctors. We initially believed that I had two, maybe three years to live and that those would be very tough years. We didn't feel that it was right to bring a baby into the world in such circumstances with the probability that I would die in the short-term. That I have been able to beat the odds so far is a bonus, but I have become increasingly ravaged by the disease. I hope you understand. Anyway, we felt so fortunate to have you that we counted our blessings every day. We still do. Because I am facing a bleak future, I concentrate on my present. You fill all of my todays with such delight. Your goodness and laughter permeate our house and our lives with enchantment and joy. Dinnertime takes more than an hour because in between mouthfuls you regale us with stories from the day. Of course, like every child, you have your moments when we threaten to put you out with the garbage or to sell you into slavery, but those times are few and far between. Honestly, we wouldn't leave you in the bin for long. You have so many of your Mother's traits; you are gentle and kind, forgiving, loyal, doggedly determined and tenacious. You have also developed a wicked sense of humour (I think that comes from my side) which brings much happiness to all those around you.

Being your Dad has been infinitely more rewarding than I could ever have imagined. Living in this useless body has allowed me the opportunity to sit and watch as your imaginative games and creative mind spring to life before me, often utilising my presence as a prop or playing a bit-part. I have observed you tenderly attending to your baby's needs (a doll, teddy or anything that remotely resembles the human form) for many hours, changing their nappies, feeding them, burping them, taking them for walks, and even chastising them when they are naughty. Each one had a name; there was Lisa, the twins Ava and Claudia, Kelly, Colleen, Molly and Alicia to name but a few.

When I came to sit in at kinder, you proudly brought all the kids up to meet me and showed them how I talked using my LightWriter. I love the fact that to you I am just a normal everyday dad, albeit with a few obvious limitations. But these don't seem to faze you – you treat me no differently, often climbing all over me as I sit in my recliner. You are also acutely aware of my needs, ready to lend a helping hand, always on the lookout for disabled parking spaces and compassionately explaining to other kids why I am the way I am. You understand better than anyone else my attempts at speech, maybe because you have grown up with my disability and have developed an ear for my voice. Children your age should not have to contend with what is served up to you on a daily basis, but you are made of tough stuff. You are special.

My worst fear is that you won't remember me when I'm gone or, at least, you won't remember me for who I really am. During quieter moments when I gazed at your picture on the wall in the year I was first diagnosed, this sense of foreboding was almost too much to bear and I would break down and cry into my hands. At that stage I believed I had only a couple of years left and that you would grow up with no memory of me but for a few vague recollections and some photographs. I longed to be abundantly more to you than that. Now that I have lived through your kindergarten years, I yearn to experience all of your school years.

Every birthday and Christmas we celebrate together is a bonus but, once joyously celebrated, I fix my attention on making it to the next, jealously hoarding every moment I can with you, etching myself further into your being. Perhaps the most oppressive of all emotions I am forced to brave is the sense that my condition is somehow restricting your opportunities to experience all that a child your age should – for that I am deeply, deeply regretful. I pray that when you read this as an adult, you won't feel that this has been the case. I pray that you will have rich, full and resonant memories of your childhood and of our time together. Mum and I try hard to maintain a sense of normality and attempt to give you everything you need but in the end, though we want to with all our hearts, we can't protect you from harsh realities, as cruel as they may be. Sometimes I am hard on you and have high expectations of your behaviour, but I make no apology for that. I know that sometimes my frown and the disapproving shake of my head irks you but I am also aware of my duties to prepare you for life. A life where self-discipline, honesty and integrity will provide solid foundations.

Every parent has aspirations and dreams for their children. I simply want you to be happy, just like you are now. Happy with who you are and what you become. Life will continue to throw many challenges at you but you are made of the right stuff to meet them, for even when you were five years old you stared adversity down, rolled up your sleeves and got on with it. I hope you continue to laugh unashamedly and hysterically, as it is in your laughter that you warm the hearts of so many people. I pray that you remain open to others, open to learning, and open to new ideas and new experiences.

Eliza, I don't know what the future holds, but I so wanted to be there for you, to watch you develop into the person I know you have the potential to become, to share in your journey and to hold your hand in times of happiness, suffering and pain. It may be that one day you get to call somebody else 'Dad' and that's a good thing - just so long as he loves and cares for you. Unfortunately, our paths lead in different directions, but I will always be walking with you – or running as you so often tend to do! Don't forget to stop every once in a while and give me a fleeting thought, maybe when you're at the beach, when you are sad or in need of help. I will never be far away – there will always be a spirit that binds us. You are a very special gift and I love you with all my heart. I always will.

You are born in love and pain.
Given to us for a short time only.
Before we must let you go again, with love and pain.
One day you'll come to know how close they are, one to the other.
You are a treasure, a blessing, a prayer's answer,
A jig in my Irish soul.
You are me, and I am you.
You are both of us, the love of your mother and me.
Let me be worthy of you.
Let me lead you to truth, to beauty, to the mystery of the universe.
You will ask me great questions, and sometimes I will not know

the answers.
Perhaps we are not meant to know some things.
That is life too...a seeking.
It may be our only purpose here.
All things are changing, always.
Yesterday is dust, tomorrow a dream.
Our gift is now.
And so, my sweet angel, may you know love, and be loved in return.
May you know truth, and laughter, and peace, and happiness,
And may the great spirit of the universe enfold you in his arms,
and keep you safe, for always.

Gabriel Byrne

Lize, I want to thank you for what you have given to me. You have made me happy beyond all measure. You have brought such joy into our lives and I love you with all my heart. I always will.

WHERE TO FIND OUT MORE
ABOUT MND

MND affects approximately 1400 people in Australia and thousands more - their carers, families and friends - live daily with its impact. On average every day in Australia at least one person dies from MND and another is diagnosed.

࿔

MND Australia
http://www.mndaust.asn.au/
MND Australia is the national peak body for MND care and research in Australia. The MND Australia network comprises of six state Associations, representing all states and territories.

MND Australia
PO Box 990
The Old Gladesville Hospital, Victoria Rd
Gladesville NSW 1675

Phone: + 61 2 9816 5322
Fax: +61 2 9816 2077
Mobile/Cell Phone: 0408 461 932
Email: info@mndaust.asn.au

MND Research Institute of Australia (MNDRIA)
http://www.mndresearch.asn.au/
The MNDRIA is the research arm of MND Australia.

PO Box 990 GLADESVILLE NSW 1675
Tel: + 61 2 8877 0990
Fax: + 61 2 9816 2077
Email: info@mndresearch.asn.au
For specific information about the MND Association providing services in your state or territory, refer to the details below or call the national freecall number: 1800 777 175

ॐ

MOTOR NEURONE DISEASE NEW SOUTH WALES INC
Building 4, Old Gladesville Hospital, Gladesville NSW 2111 (Locked Bag 5005, Gladesville NSW 1675)
Telephone: (02) 8877 0999
Fax: (02) 9816 2077
Freecall: 1800 777 175
Email: admin@mndnsw.asn.au

ॐ

MOTOR NEURONE DISEASE QUEENSLAND INC
PO Box 259, Corinda Qld 4075
Telephone: (07) 3372 9004
Fax: (07) 3278 9871
Freecall: 1800 777 175
Email: info@mndaq.org.au

❧

MOTOR NEURONE DISEASE SOUTH AUSTRALIA INC
302 South Road Hilton SA 5033.
(PO Box 2087, Hilton Plaza SA 5033)
Telephone: (08) 8234 8448
Fax: (08) 8152 0447
Freecall: 1800 777 175
Email: admin@mndasa.com.au

❧

MOTOR NEURONE DISEASE TASMANIA INC
PO Box 379, Sandy Bay TAS 7006
Freecall: 1800 777 175 or 1800 806 632
Email: info@mndatas.asn.au

❧

MOTOR NEURONE DISEASE VICTORIA INC
265 Canterbury Rd, (PO Box 23) Canterbury Vic 3126
Telephone: (03) 9830 2122
Fax: (03) 9830 2228
Freecall: 1800 806 632
Email: info@mnd.asn.au

∽⌒∾

MOTOR NEURONE DISEASE WESTERN AUSTRALIA INC
Centre for Neurological Support –
The Niche, B/11 Aberdare Rd, Nedlands WA 6009
Telephone: (08) 9346 7355
Fax: (08) 9346 7332
Freecall: 1800 777 175
Email: admin@mndawa.asn.au

SILENT BODY
VIBRANT MIND

Living with Motor Neurone Disease

Peter Anderson

ISBN 9781922036506   Qty

RRP   AU$24.99   .....

Postage within Australia   AU$5.00   .....

TOTAL★ $_____

★ All prices include GST

Name: ....

Address: ....

....

Phone:...

Email: ....

Payment: ❏ Money Order ❏ Cheque ❏ Amex ❏ MasterCard ❏ Visa

Cardholders Name:...

Credit Card Number: ....

Signature:...

Expiry Date: ....

Allow 21 days for delivery.

Payment to: Better Bookshop (ABN 14 067 257 390)
                          PO Box 12544
                          A'Beckett Street, Melbourne, 8006
                          Victoria, Australia
                          Fax: +61 3 9671 4730
                          betterbookshop@brolgapublishing.com.au

BE PUBLISHED

Publishing through a successful Australian publisher. Brolga provides:

- Editorial appraisal
- Cover design
- Typesetting
- Printing
- Author promotion
- National book trade distribution, including sales, marketing and distribution through Macmillan Australia.
- International book trade distribution
- Worldwide e-book distribution

For details and inquiries, contact:
Brolga Publishing Pty Ltd
PO Box 12544
A'Beckett St VIC 8006

Phone: 0414 608 494
admin@brolgapublishing.com.au
markzocchi@brolgapublishing.com.au
ABN: 46 063 962 443